Portland Community College

D0465132

Knowing the Enemy

Knowing

the

Enemy

Jihadist Ideology and the War on Terror

Mary R. Habeck

YALE UNIVERSITY PRESS   NEW HAVEN & LONDON

Designed by Rebecca Gibb.
Set in Janson text type by Integrated Publishing Solutions.
Printed in the United States of America.

Library of Congress Cataloging-in-Publication Data
Habeck, Mary R.
Knowing the enemy : jihadist ideology and the War on Terror / Mary R. Habeck.
p. cm.
Includes bibliographical references and index.
ISBN 0-300-11306-4 (hardcover : alk. paper)
1. Terrorism—Religious aspects—Islam. 2. Islam and world politics. 3. War
on Terrorism, 2001–. I. Title.
BP190.5.T47H33 2006
297.2'72—dc22   2005015210

A catalogue record for this book is available from the British Library.

The paper in this book meets the guidelines for permanence and durability
of the Committee on Production Guidelines for Book Longevity
of the Council on Library Resources.

10 9 8 7 6 5 4 3

Contents

1 Why They Did It 1

2 Historical Context 17

3 The Qur'an Is Our Constitution 41

4 Our *'Aqida* 57

5 The Clash of Civilizations, Part I:
The American Campaign to Suppress Islam 83

6 The Clash of Civilizations, Part II:
Jihad on the Path of God 107

7 From Mecca to Medina:
Following the Method of Muhammad 135

Contents

8 Jihadist Ideology and the War on Terror 161

NOTES 179

GLOSSARY 233

INDEX 237

Knowing the Enemy

1 *Why They Did It*

Immediately after September 11, 2001, Americans agonized over the reason why nineteen men hated the United States enough to kill three thousand civilians in an unprovoked assault. The list of explanations offered by analysts and scholars was long and varied—U.S. policies in the Middle East (most especially America's support for Israel), globalization, U.S. arrogance, imperialism (cultural, political, and economic), and the poverty and oppression endemic in many Arab countries were all blamed as the root causes for the attacks. Other observers, like President George W. Bush, argued that it was the very existence of the United States that led to the attacks. In this view certain nations and people fear and envy what they do not have for themselves—the freedoms, democracy, power, and wealth of the

United States—and this alone is enough to explain why the towers had to fall.

Among all these explanations the one voice missing was that of the attackers themselves: what were the reasons that they gave for the attack? Their deaths should not prevent us from listening to them, because they belong to a larger extremist group that has not been shy about sharing its views with the entire world. To understand "why they hate us" we therefore need first to know where to look and who listen to: our first question must not be "why do they hate America?" but "*who* is it that hates America enough to kill?" Not all Arabs and not all Muslims chose to carry out the attacks, but rather a particular type of militant with specific views about a need to resort to violence. Knowing who these people are, and what their views are, we will then be able to hear what they themselves say and why they decided to kill as many Americans as possible that September day.

Any answer to this initial question must acknowledge the fact that the hijackers were Muslims and that al-Qaida, the group they were associated with, claimed to carry out the attacks in the name of Islam. But we must be clear about the relationship between these men and the religion of Islam. Just as not all Muslims deliberately murdered three thousand innocents in New York City, Washington, D.C., and rural Pennsylvania, it would also be misguided—even evil—to suggest that all Muslims desired the deaths that happened that day. Indeed, though demonstrations in support of the hijackers and protests against U.S.

policies have occurred since, the "Muslim street" has not risen, taken up arms, and attacked America. The few thousand extremists who are fighting U.S. troops in Afghanistan and Iraq pale in comparison to the bloodshed that would occur if the entire Islamic community decided to kill Americans.

Yet it would be just as wrong to conclude that the hijackers, al-Qaida, and the other radical groups have nothing to do with Islam. As we shall see, these extremists explicitly appeal to the holy texts (the Qur'an and *sunna*, as laid out in the *hadith*) to show that their actions are justified. They find, too, endorsement of their ideas among respected interpreters of Islam and win disciples by their piety and their sophisticated arguments about how the religion supports them. The question is *which* Islam they represent. As the religion of over a billion people, Islam does not present a united face, and it is practiced in a variety of ways: syncretistic forms in Indonesia and Africa; traditional beliefs in rural areas of central Asia, Egypt, Iran, and North Africa; secularized variants in Tunisia, Iraq, Syria, and Turkey; and mystical Sufi sects, which dominate large swathes of the Muslim world. None of these versions of Islam—which encompass the vast majority of the world's Muslims—have called for a war against the United States. To blame "Islam"—full stop—for September 11 is not only wrongheaded, it is ultimately self-defeating in the struggle that confronts America. By lumping Muslims into one undifferentiated mass it threatens to radicalize the more than billion believers who do not want the United States destroyed.

Some analysts have suggested that the attackers should be identified with "fundamentalism" or "Islamism," the reforming Islam that calls for a revival of the religion and a "return" of Islam to political power. But Islamism likewise represents neither a unified nor uniform phenomenon. The term describes, rather, a complex of often antagonistic groups with differing beliefs, goals, and methodologies for attaining their ends. Some of these groups (such as Turkey's Justice and Development Party [the AK]) are committed to democratic processes and to the international system. To identify parties like the AK with the terrorists of 9/11 threatens to confuse rather than clarify the situation. It prevents a differentiation between Islamists with whom one can hold discourse and work with as friends and allies, and the armed gangs who may need to be dealt with through force.

This book will argue that the nineteen men who attacked the United States and the many other groups who continue to work for its destruction—including al-Qaida—are part of a radical faction of the multifaceted Islamist belief system. This faction— generally called "jihadi" or "jihadist"—has very specific views about how to revive Islam, how to return Muslims to political power, and what needs to be done about its enemies, including the United States. The main difference between jihadis and other Islamists is the extremists' commitment to the violent overthrow of the existing international system and its replacement by an all-encompassing Islamic state. To justify their resort to violence, they define "jihad" (a term that can mean an internal struggle to please God as well as an external battle to open countries to the call of Islam) as fighting alone.[1] Only by understanding the elaborate ideology of the jihadist faction can the United States, as well as the rest of the world, determine how to contain and eventually end the threat they pose to stability and peace.

Some might object that nationality, social factors, and historical processes are more important than religion in explaining the larger motives of these hijackers and their reasons for carrying out their attack. All nineteen men were Arabs, and fifteen of them even came from one country, Saudi Arabia—surely, supporters of this view argue, such factors must account for their involvement in this heinous act. Public intellectuals such as Edward Said, and experts like Tariq Ali and Tariq Ramadan, have concluded that the colonization of Islamic lands and their (often) forcible Westernization–modernization is cause enough for the radicals to strike out at the United States. In these analyses religion is taken as epiphenomenal; economic, political, and social factors are seen as the basis for any serious explication of the extremists' actions. The argument of this book, however, is that all these factors (nationality, poverty, oppressive governments, colonization, imperialism) only partially explain a commitment to extremist religious groups. These are important underlying issues that may push Muslims toward some sort of violent reaction, but they do not, by themselves, explain why jihadis have chosen to turn to violence now, and why the extremists offer religious explanations for all their actions. Muhammad Atta and the other eighteen men who took part in the September 11 attacks were middle-class and well-educated, and had bright futures ahead of them. They participated in the hijackings not because they were forced to do so through sudden economic or social deprivation, but because they chose to deal with the problems of their community—for religious/ideological reasons—by killing as many Americans as they could. Explanations that focus on the negative effects of colonization require similar qualification. Although colonization was certainly a traumatic experience for the Middle East (as it was for the rest of the colonized world), its impact again explains neither the timing nor shape of the current extremism. If the entire purpose of jihadism is to break an imperial stranglehold on the Islamic world—symbolized by U.S. support for Israel—why did the U.S. become the focus of Sayyid Qutb's anger in the early 1950s (more than a decade before the United States became associated with Israel)? Moreover, how do the effects of colonization account for the fact that one of the earliest jihadist thinkers, Muhammad ibn 'Abd al-Wahhab, developed his version of radical and violent Islam long before the West colonized Islamic lands, indeed at a time when Islam seemed triumphant? Other Islamic extremists in Africa, men like Usman dan Fodio, Muhammad al-Jaylani, and Shehu Ahmadu Lobbo began jihads aimed at restoring "true" Islam before Europeans became a factor in West Africa. Meanwhile Shah Wali Allah articulated a new vision of forcing Islam on Hindus for their own good—through jihad—at the very same time as Wahhab was preaching his version of offensive jihad against apostate Muslims.

The consistent need to find explanations other than religious ones for the attacks says, in fact, more about the West than it does about the jihadis. Western scholars have generally failed to take religion seriously. Secularists, whether liberals or socialists, grant true explanatory power to political, social, or economic factors but discount the plain sense of religious statements made by the jihadis themselves. To see why jihadis declared war on the United States and tried to kill as many Americans as possible, we must be willing to listen to their own explanations. To do otherwise is to impose a Western interpretation on the extremists, in effect to listen to ourselves rather than to them.

How do the jihadis explain their actions? They say that they are committed to the destruction of the entire secular world because they believe this is a necessary first step to create an Islamic utopia on earth. The chain of thought that leads to this conclusion is complicated and uses reasoning that anyone outside the extremist camp may find hard to fathom. This, as we may expect, matters little to the jihadis. They do not care if their assertions find resonance within any community other than their own, and they use concepts, symbols, and familiar events that appeal to discontented Muslims, not to outsiders. It is also worth emphasizing that they play fast and loose with both historical fact and traditional religious interpretation in order to understand their past as they believe it must be understood. First, they argue that Islam is meant to be the only way of life for humanity. After earlier versions of the one true religion had become corrupted by willful men, God sent down to mankind the Qur'an and Muhammad to show people how to please Him and how to create the perfect society. The Muslims were those men and women who submitted to Him and His law, and their community (*umma*) was told that they were divinely destined to lead mankind.[2] Once Muslims were given the Truth, it was now their duty to share with others the way to divine favor and the ideal society. If prevented by unrighteous rulers from doing so, they must fight (wage jihad) to open the country for the call to Islam. In addition, since Islam is a message meant to create a community of believers, jihadis argue that Muslims must live in a society that implements all the laws commanded by God—and as lived out by Muhammad and explained by the learned men of religion (the *ulama*). Not even the least of the ordinances of God can be ignored or flouted. In their vision of history, Muslims did as they were commanded for over a thousand years, spreading the true faith, creating a unified society (the Caliphate, or *Khilafa*) that followed the law system given by God (the *shari'a*), and in return were granted the right to rule the world, dispensing justice and calling people out of darkness and into light.[3]

Then, in the jihadist account, something went terribly wrong with this God-ordained order. Christians and Jews, followers of the corrupted religions, somehow became the new leaders of mankind and began to dictate to Muslims how they should live. The Christian Europeans even conquered and occupied Islamic territory and created Israel as a permanent bridgehead in the lands of the umma. Meanwhile, the United States, Europe, and even Japan and other Asian states developed militarily, economically, and politically into superpowers that dominated international politics, finance, the media, popular culture—in sum, all of human life. Every day the community of true believers is publicly humiliated, reminded that it is powerless and ruled by the unbelievers rather than ruling them. These are the "inversed facts," the predicament that has left nothing in its "right place," and has "turned life inside out," making the umma a "dead nation."[4]

How did this terrible situation come about? Jihadist ideologues offer three basic explanations. One locates the problem in the earliest years of Islam, after the four righteous Caliphs (*al-Rashidun*) were replaced by a hereditary monarchy under the Abbasids. This unlawful system of government led to a variety of intellectual, religious, and political ills.[5] Politically and religiously, the new monarchy gave rise to despotic rulers who created their own laws rather than implement the God-given law system of shari'a. The jihadis argue that these tyrants, by ruling with their own laws, actually dethroned God and set themselves up as divine in his place. Today the tyrants still exist—Mubarak, Musharraf, Assad, and the Saudis are all the spiritual heirs of those first hereditary rulers—and are supported in their apostasy by the United States and other Western countries, which use them as their puppets to undermine Islam and destroy God's laws on earth. Intellectually, jihadis argue that the Abbasids brought an end to reason (*ijtihad*) as a way to adapt Islamic beliefs to changing circumstances. In this view Islamic scholars, until the age of the Abbasids, had the ability to creatively interpret the sacred texts. By imposing one particular school of jurisprudence as the official interpretation of Islam, these Caliphs destroyed the ability of the Muslim nation to react to new threats and challenges.[6] Precisely the opposite argument is made by most modern scholars, who note that the Abbasids and the Caliphs who followed them attempted to integrate Greek thought into Islam, thus opening the door for human reason to supplement divine revelation. The jihadis will have none of this argument, since for them the intermixing of Greek and Western ideas with Islam only further polluted an already weakened religion. The overthrow of the Abbasids did not undo the damage, for a few hundred years later Islamic jurists announced that they had decided every important legal question, and that therefore "the gates of ijtihad were closed." After that, Muslims were told they could only seek out a learned religious leader and follow his example.[7] Blind imitation led to the stagnation and inflexibility of the Ottoman Empire and, when faced with the challenge of a resurgent Europe, the eventual destruction of Islam as a thriving civilization. The solution of jihadis to this intellectual stagnation is a return to the Qur'an and hadith alone as the only authorities for their actions. They want to eliminate interpretations and traditions that they see as heretical and, using their own reason, justify their conduct through the sacred texts alone.

Other jihadis believe that the trouble began on 3 March 1924, when Mustafa Kemal Atatürk abolished the Ottoman Caliphate—the religious ruler seen as the only authority for all of Islam. That act, called "the mother of all crimes" by one jihadist professor, spelled an end to "true" Islam.[8] Despite the overwhelming evidence to the contrary, jihadis assert that since the death of Muhammad there had existed only one Caliph at a time who ruled the entire community of believers. It was the duty of the Caliph to guard the Muslims, lead them into battle with the infidels, and make certain that good deeds were promoted and evil deeds prevented. Since only under a Caliph recognized by the entire Muslim nation could the shari'a be fully implemented, the abolition of the Caliphate destroyed Islam. Sayyid Qutb, the main ideologue of modern jihadist groups, argued that this crime meant that so-called Muslims had been living in sin since 1924 and that Islam was no longer being practiced anywhere in the world.[9]

Finally there are jihadis who believe that Muslims lost their dignity and honor through a deliberate assault by "unbelief" on Islam.[10] Since the beginning of time falsehood (*batil*) and unbelief (*kufr*), envisioned as purely evil forces that take on different forms depending on the epoch, have attempted to destroy the one true faith. With the coming of the last prophet, Muhammad, the conflict between the two sharpened into outright warfare. At that time kufr was represented by the unbelieving Jews and Christians who rejected Islam. For over 1,400 years the war raged, with the "Truth" always able to win out in the end, even when Christian crusaders invaded the Muslim homeland in a futile attempt to destroy Islam. Then the latest embodiments of unbelief, Europe and America (still representing the crusaders and the Jews), managed to weaken the umma as none of the other forms of unbelief had—colonizing their lands and humiliating them before the entire world.[11] In contrast to Western critics of colonialism, who attribute European imperialism to capitalism, power politics, or greed, the jihadis argue that religion alone explains this hostility. The entire purpose of imperialism was, in this view, to destroy Islam and kill as many Muslims as possible. The decline of Islam is thus not mainly the result of internal weaknesses or sin by the Muslims themselves, but is rather the deliberate policy of an external religious enemy whom jihadis can—and do—blame for all the evils suffered by Muslims around the world.

In many ways, the course of action chosen to correct the ills that have befallen Islam and Muslim societies depends upon which of these explanations a particular jihadist group prefers. All jihadis agree that Muslims must "open the doors of ijtihad," allowing every individual to interpret the sacred texts through his own reason (informed by the interpretations of respected ulama) rather than blind imitation. The result is the overthrow of 1,400 years of development in Islamic law and theology, the rejection of any interpretations but those that fit into the preconceived notions of the jihadis, and the creation of hundreds of splinter groups, each convinced that it alone knows the truth about the faith. After these few points of agreement, jihadist groups differ significantly about strategies to return Islam to greatness. Those jihadis who locate the problem in the offenses of Muslims themselves, and particularly in the evil system of monarchy represented today by the rulers in every Islamic country, talk openly about killing these "agents of the West" and replacing them with men who will rule by the shari'a alone. The jihadis who see the destruction of the Caliphate as the essence of the problem want to recreate an all-encompassing Islamic state (not just one in any individual country), and then go on to conquer the rest of the world for Islam. The group most associated with this view, Hizb al-Tahrir, while refusing to engage in offensive warfare itself until the "restoration" of the Caliphate, nonetheless spends much of its energy inciting Muslims to violence and promoting a defensive jihad to expel the unbelievers. Other jihadis see Europe, the United States, and the Jews—collectively viewed as the modern representative of "unbelief" and "falsehood"—as the sole reason for their decline. To solve their internal problems (poverty, tyrannical governments, and lack of military power), and to end the oppression and aggression of the West, they have decided to concentrate on the destruction of one or the other of these "eternal" enemies.

The September 11 attackers belong to this last category. For these jihadis, fighting under the banner of al-Qaida, the attack on the United States was required of them as defenders of the "true" faith. Al-Qaida believed that the United States, as the greatest representative of "unbelief," had to be struck a stunning blow, killing as many Americans as possible to frighten the U.S. government into submission (as earlier blows in Beirut and Somalia had), and to begin the ultimate destruction of falsehood around the world. Once the United States had left Islamic lands, ending its "occupation" of Arabia and retreating behind its own borders, they intended to turn their violence upon the unjust rulers of Muslim countries, beginning with the Saudis. After the tyrants had fallen, they would take up the warfare by Islam against the rest of the world—a battle that they believe colonialism interrupted. Al-Qaida hoped as well to provoke the United States into an unconsidered response that would unite the entire Islamic world behind their vision of eternal warfare against the unbelievers.[12] In many ways, then, the attacks of September 11 were as much about convincing other Muslims to join the extremists in their war as it was about killing Americans.

There are, of course, numerous parts of this explanation that make little or no sense to an outside observer. To understand why September 11 happened, and what the jihadis are likely to do in the future, the reader must be willing to suspend cultural and intellectual preconceptions and become submerged in the mindset of the extremists. In this world, historical facts do not matter, nor do the realities of power balances (military, economic, political, and diplomatic). What is important to the jihadis is getting the fundamentals of life "right." Once the believers understand these basic principles, and act correctly upon them, everything else will fall into place. In concrete terms jihadis believe that their mission is to implement their version of Islam, including the imperative to carry out warfare against the unbelievers, and all the troubles of the Islamic world will disappear.

Faced with this acutely religious sensibility, the United States, and the West in general, must be willing to lay aside prejudices and be open to hearing what the jihadis themselves are saying. They are telling everyone in the world what they believe and how they will act. The question is whether anyone is listening to them.

2 *Historical Context*

The ideas supported by the jihadis did not spring from a void, nor are all of them the marginal opinions of a few fanatics. The principle dogmas that they assert—that Islam is the one true faith that will dominate the world; that Muslim rulers need to govern by the shari'a alone; that the Qur'an and hadith contain the whole truth for determining the righteous life; that there is no separation between religion and the rest of life; and that Muslims are in a state of conflict with the unbelievers—have roots in discussions about Islamic law and theology that began soon after the death of Muhammad and that are supported by important segments of the clergy (ulama) today. Scholars have also traced the evolution of even the more extreme jihadist beliefs from the interpretations of Ahmad ibn 'Abd al-Halim Ibn Taymiyya (1263–1328), through the thought of Muhammad ibn

'Abd al-Wahhab (1703/4–1792), Muhammad Rashid Rida (1865–1935), Hasan al-Banna (1906–1949), Sayyid Abul A'la Mawdudi (1903–1979), and Sayyid Qutb (1903–1966).[1]

This is not to suggest that jihadis have been uninfluenced by current political, social, and cultural events in the Islamic world and by the interaction of that world with Europe and the United States over the last two centuries. The experiences of colonization and decolonization, and the twin ideas of nationalism and socialism, have especially impacted the development of jihadist ideology, while the global phenomenon of modernization has affected the Islamic community as much as it has the rest of the world. However, it is to religion—however misused and abused—that the jihadis regularly appeal when talking about their beliefs or explaining their actions. They mention other issues (especially imperialism, nationalism, and socialism) but from a purely religious viewpoint, and they draw conclusions about how Muslims should respond to them from the Qur'an, hadith, and the life of Muhammad. Jihadist ideologues who use words like "capitalism," "women's liberation," and "human rights" empty them of the meanings that they usually have in Europe and America and fill them with an Islamicized significance. To ignore the justifications offered by jihadis themselves for what they do is a fatal mistake, because they claim to have chosen every strategy, tactic, and target in their war with the United States based on religious principles. It is also terribly insulting, for it denigrates their own explanations of motives and privileges Western notions of reasonable beliefs over theirs.

The modern Islamists and jihadis alike assert that they draw their primary inspiration from Ibn Taymiyya, a widely respected interpreter of the Qur'an and sunna (prophetic tradition).[2] His writing is, significantly, acknowledged as a valid interpretation of the shari'a (Islamic law) by other Muslims, and springs from the Hanbali school, one of the four orthodox schools of Islamic jurisprudence (*fiqh*) that are recognized and followed by Sunni Muslims around the world.[3] It was Ibn Taymiyya who persuasively argued that Islam requires state power, the foundational principle for all Islamists. Living at a time when shamanist Mongols had conquered the core of the Islamic world, he issued religious rulings which decreed that Muslims could not live in a nation ruled by infidels. A more complicated situation was presented by Mongol rulers who claimed to be Muslims and yet continued to use their native system of laws—the *yasa*—to make judgments. Ibn Taymiyya asserted that these rulers were acting immorally and contrary to the Qur'anic text, which said that Muslims were only truly the "best community" when they "enjoined the good and forbade the evil." This injunction he took to mean that Muslims had to follow and implement all the commandments, both positive and negative, laid down by God and explained by Muhammad (and as interpreted by the legal experts); not the least of them could be ignored or disobeyed.[4] Ibn Taymiyya argued that since the Mongol rulers failed to carry out the entire shari'a of God and even pretended that their own system of law was superior in certain regards, they were not fulfilling this key requirement. Such rulers were clearly infidels and not Muslims at all, and as unbelievers had to be fought and killed.[5]

Given the times in which he lived, it should come as no surprise that Ibn Taymiyya also supported the resumption of armed struggle against anyone outside the fold of Islam. He would, in fact, become known as one of the foremost proponents of the Islamic duty called "jihad." It seems appropriate to stop here and attempt to understand this difficult concept before going further. Jihad is derived from the Arabic root for "struggle" and not from the usual word for war.[6] This gives a clue to the significance that the Qur'an and the hadith assign to it, for jihad was never meant to be warfare for the sake of national or personal gain, but rather struggle for the sake of God and on His path alone. Jihad thus has two basic meanings: the first deals with the internal struggle to follow God and do all that He has commanded. The second is to engage in an external struggle (fighting) with others to bring the Truth (Islam) to mankind. Jihad was never supposed to be about the forcible conversion of others to Islam—although under some rulers it became that—but rather about opening the doors to countries so that the oppressed peoples within could hear the Truth and, once Muslims conquered the land, have the privilege of being ruled by the just laws of Islam. The best way to translate "jihad" is therefore not "holy war" but rather "just war"—a war that is justified for Muslims because it is meant to free other people from falsehood and lead them to truth.

It is jihad as fighting that has historically dominated discussions of the duty in Islamic law and that also dominates in the writings of Ibn Taymiyya. He called jihad the "best of all the voluntary (good actions) which man performs," even better than the hajj.[7] This is a bold statement, for traditionally the hajj is considered one of the five duties obligatory for every Muslim who can afford it. In another place he equated jihad with the love of God, writing that "Jihad involves absolute love for that which Allah has commanded and absolute hatred for that which He has forbidden, and so whom He loves and who love Him is '. . . lowly with the Believers, mighty against the Rejecters, fighting in the Way of Allah and never afraid of the reproaches of such as find fault.'"[8] Ibn Taymiyya also broadened the definition of jihadic activity, creating one of the first serious reconsiderations of the obligation since the time of Muhammad. After a careful study of the relevant traditions and Qur'anic passages, he concluded that not only should the Islamic nation fight all heretics, apostates, hypocrites, sinners, and unbelievers (including Christians and Jews) until "all religion was for God alone," but also any Muslim who tried to avoid participating in jihad.[9] His theory about jihad—its significance, necessity, and types of fighting that should be included within its realm—was one of the major contributions that Ibn Taymiyya made to Islamic law.

Ibn Taymiyya's thought finds resonance with jihadist groups, for their ideologues believe that there are significant similarities between the situation faced by the jurist eight hundred years ago and the one that they confront today. Just as in the thirteenth century, Islamic lands were conquered and ruled by unbelievers. Although the infidels have been expelled, and the current rulers of Islamic countries say that they are Muslims, like the Mongols they use laws other than the shari'a to govern. This in the minds of the jihadis makes the present leaders of every Islamic country the infidels that Ibn Taymiyya called such rulers, and they must be fought against and killed if they do not repent. For the jihadis, Ibn Taymiyya's rulings in fact provide the legal grounds for their attempts to overthrow Islamic political leaders.[10] Ibn Taymiyya's views of just war also give jihadis the necessary legitimacy to carry out offensive and defensive warfare against unbelievers and "apostate," "heretical," and "sinning" Muslims alike.[11]

Nearly five hundred years after Ibn Taymiyya, Muhammad ibn 'Abd al-Wahhab revived these arguments and added vital touches of his own.[12] By the beginning of the eighteenth century, the Ottoman Empire had entered a difficult period of military, economic, and technological stagnation. The territorial expansion of its first few centuries ground to a halt, and the Ottomans suffered a series of setbacks at the hands of various European powers. Meanwhile, strong leaders in a number of peripheral provinces began to struggle for greater independence from the central authorities.[13] Wahhab, like Ibn Taymiyya a jurist of the Hanbali tradition, was able to take advantage of the problems that the Ottomans faced to implement a vision of Islam influenced by Ibn Taymiyya and yet uniquely his own.[14] When his first attempts at convincing other Muslims to follow him led only to exile, Wahhab made a fateful alliance with the Saudi family that would spread his vision of "true" Islam across the Arabian peninsula and beyond.

Wahhab's argument began with the proposition that believers had to learn to think for themselves and to reject the blind imitation of the clerics. In his vision of Islam, a Muslim was not obliged to follow anyone except God and Muhammad; the Qur'an and sunna were supreme.[15] From his own study and reasoning about the holy texts, Wahhab concluded that most Muslims did not understand or practice correctly the central tenet of Islam. This doctrine, *tawhid*, is the belief that God is one and that He has no partners: the founding principle of Islam and the point of departure for the entire religion. Wahhab asserted that there were in fact three sorts of tawhid, and that Muslims had to acknowledge all three and live them out in their lives, or they were not truly Muslims. One of these sorts of tawhid—that of God's lordship—is particularly interesting for our further discussion.[16] Wahhab argued that since God alone was lord, and that He could have no associates or partners who shared this divine attribute, all matters of ruling and lawgiving belonged to Him uniquely. No human being could make laws or alter in any way the shari'a that He had granted to mankind, for to do so was to set oneself up as a god in the place of the true divinity. Like

Ibn Taymiyya, Wahhab prescribed jihad against these wicked heretics as the only Islamic solution for their evil.

Wahhab proposed another sort of tawhid as well—the uniqueness of God's worship.[17] Because only God is worthy of worship, any objects or people that are entreated, that have prayers directed at them, or that are given any of His attributes have taken His place. Any Muslim who engages in this sort of activity has become an unbeliever and should be treated as such, that is, fought and killed. This concept has led to some of what is often called the "puritanism" of his followers, generally called Wahhabis: the smashing of images, tombs, and saints' shrines.[18] The destruction of the Bamyan Buddhas by the Taliban—who were strongly influenced by Wahhabi preachers—is a logical expression of this belief, as was the decision by the Saudis to destroy the tombs of even Muhammad's earliest companions. Part of the antipathy shown by Wahhabis (in Saudi Arabia and other countries where they have held power) toward both Sufis and the Shiʻa flows from the latter's veneration and supplication of saints (pirs) as well as the high position given to Shiʻa clergy and to ʻAli and his relatives (for the Shiʻa the main religious figures for imitation after Muhammad). The similarities with Ibn Taymiyya's thought are too striking to be mere coincidence, and it comes as no surprise that Wahhab was also a Hanbali, had studied Ibn Taymiyya thoroughly, and used his work as the basis for much of his theology.

Some jihadis have been greatly influenced by Wahhab's interpretations of Islam, even when they do not quote him directly.[19]

His ideas about the "true" meaning of tawhid reappear in the writings of Sayyid Qutb and other ideologues, while his disdain for Sufism and Shi'ism may explain the actions of those few jihadis (like Zarqawi and the Taliban) who have managed to take power even over small pieces of territory. Jihadist groups that do not specifically mention Wahhab in explaining their beliefs also share certain characteristics with the jurist—his resorting to violence to establish his ideas even when it meant killing other Muslims, his intolerance for innovative interpretations of the holy texts, and his desire to convert all Muslims to his own beliefs—that justify calling them Wahhabi-influenced if not outright "Wahhabi."

But Wahhab's ideology had little impact on the great currents of Islamic thought during the nineteenth and early twentieth centuries. For nearly two hundred years, his ideas were marginalized expressions of the religion, shared by few Muslims outside the Arabian peninsula. As Hamid Algar points out, it would be a mistake then to see a direct line and connection between Wahhabism and the later salafi movements. Instead, Wahhab's ideas would come to influence the modern "Islamic Awakening," when individual Muslims migrated to Saudi Arabia for employment during the sixties and seventies and there were exposed to his thought, and when the oil shocks of the seventies gave Wahhabi preachers millions of petrodollars to spread their version of Islam throughout the world.[20] The numerous revival movements that sprang up during the eighteenth and early nineteenth centuries did, however, share one characteristic with that of Wahhab: they too had little to do with external pressures from Europeans or other invaders and much more to do with the internal dynamics of Islamic countries.[21] Ibn Taymiyya also sank into relative obscurity, his thought not seen as relevant for dealing with the problems that the Islamic world faced. Yet his ideas were kept alive by a succession of Hanbali theologians and jurists, ready to be used when certain Muslims found themselves in a situation they would perceive as similar to that of the thirteenth century.[22]

Then Europeans, mostly absent from Islamic history since the last crusaders left the Levant in the thirteenth century, returned to the lands of the umma. Parts of the East Indies had long been under European influence, but when Egypt fell to Napoleon's army in 1798 a central part of the traditional Arab–Muslim universe came under foreign control for the first time since the crusades. Throughout the nineteenth century Islamic territory fell piece by piece to one European country or another. When the final remnants of the Ottoman Empire were divided up as French and British mandates after the First World War, all Islamic lands except Turkey proper were under European rule. The response of Muslims to this unequal contact with Western nations ran the gamut from outright rejection and resistance to embracing the ideas and ideals of Europe. Islamic intellectuals in particular were prompted to reform and modernize their religion after contacts with the imperialism of France, Britain, Germany, and Italy. Here, though, there was a split as well. Some clergy and jurists agreed with a common European diagnosis of their ills: that traditional interpretations of Islam—especially notions of women's roles in society, support for polygamy and slavery, and blind following of the clergy—had to be changed drastically to fit into the modern era. Concepts like secularization, the separation of religion and state, materialism, nationalism, and liberalism made sense to these men and formed the basis for their ideologies of modernization. Other Islamic scholars were convinced that Islam itself, and especially a revival of the "true" Islam of their righteous predecessors (the *Salaf*—and thus their general name, *salafi*), would empower their community to throw off European dominion and return to greatness.

This seminal divide defined the great debate between modernizers and revivalists that would last the entire twentieth century. For our purposes, it is important that those men of religion who supported a return to Islam and the "true" Islamic principles of the past would at first lose the argument. The early twentieth century is dominated by modernists of various stripes: nationalists, socialists, and liberals, who would help to create the modern nations of the Islamic world. Meanwhile the revivalists, men such as Muhammad Rashid Rida, Hassan al-Banna, and Sayyid Abul A'la Mawdudi, continued to refine their ideas about how Islam could solve the twin problems of modernity and foreign domination. Rida is an interesting transitional figure, beginning as a modernizer and only later in life returning to Islam as the answer for the ills of the umma. Heavily influenced by the two most prominent reformers of the nineteenth century, Sayyid Jamal al-Din al-Afghani and Muhammad 'Abduh, Rashid Rida at first supported the attempts of Muslim scholars to transform their religious faith to meet the demands of modernity. But by the 1920s he began to retreat from this position, arguing that attempts to change Islam had gone too far. Muslims were losing their faith and neglecting the practice of their religion, while the liberation of women and other social reforms were destroying the very fabric of Islamic society.[23] Rida urged Muslims to stop imitating the foreigners and following their ways, and called the Islamic modernizers "false renewers" and "heretics." He condemned the Turks for the secularization of their country, and especially excoriated the scholars who provided religious rulings to support these "heretical" ways. When Mustafa Kemal Atatürk ended the Caliphate Rida would write that Islam "does not really exist unless an independent and strong Islamic State is established which could apply the laws of Islam and defend it against any foreign opposition and domination."[24] He eventually became an admirer of Wahhabism, argued that the Qur'an and sunna were sufficient to define all of existence, and that Muslims should follow only the example of the Salaf.[25] Perhaps even more importantly, Rida was the first modern revivalist to "rediscover" Ibn Taymiyya and apply the Mongol analogy to the present day dilemma of the Islamic world.[26]

During the mid-twentieth century three ideologues would take the ideas of Ibn Taymiyya, Wahhab, and Rida and transform them into a coherent set of beliefs about Islam, politics, and warfare. Their thought is by far the most significant source for jihadist ideology as well as for other, less radical, expressions of Islamism. Here we will note only the most significant aspects of their thought—later chapters will explore their ideas, and their connections to modern jihadis, in greater depth. Al-Banna, Mawdudi, and Qutb were born within three years of each other, at the dawning of the twentieth century. Al-Banna, an Egyptian, was profoundly affected by the British occupation and domination of his country as well as by the general collapse of Islamic power, and he would dedicate his entire life to solving both these issues. Although he would draw the majority of his thinking from Islam and Islamic sources, and though he was especially influenced by Rida, al-Banna did not ignore modern European concepts like nationalism, patriotism, constitutionalism, and socialism in his search for an answer.[27] But al-Banna did not accept foreign ideas as they had been defined by the West—rather he gave to them an Islamic meaning and showed how they could be transformed to conform with the Qur'an and hadith. For instance, he wrote, "If [Europeans] mean by 'patriotism' the conquest of countries and lordship over the earth, Islam has already ordained that, and has sent out conquerors to carry out the most gracious of colonizations and the most blessed of conquests. This is what He, the Almighty, says: 'Fight them till there is no longer discord, and the religion is God's.'"[28] As we shall see, Mawdudi, Qutb, and later jihadist ideologues would routinely empty European ideas like capitalism, socialism, and women's liberation of their original meanings and redefine them to make them compatible with their visions of Islam.[29]

One of al-Banna's contributions to Islamist (and jihadist) thought was his recognition of Europe (and the West) as an intellectual as well as physical threat—one that Muslims had to combat on both levels.[30] Intellectually, he called for an end to Westernization and the "mental colonization" of Muslims. He was especially disturbed by the impact that Western-style education, part of this social struggle carried out against Islam by the West, had on Muslims.[31] Up to his time the West had won out in the "ruthless war whose battlefield has been the spirits and souls of Muslims as well as their beliefs and intellects, exactly as it has triumphed on the political and military battlefields."[32] But now the umma would go through a social reformation that flowed from the basics of the religion and their application to everyday life. Islam, he argued, had to proclaim the unity of Muslims and the brotherhood of man, safeguard society (and rights to property, education, just profits, and more) while controlling the instincts for food and sex, and punishing infractions the Islamic way.[33] Only through a proper Islamic education could Muslims relearn how to do all this, and only through social work could they be applied in actual life. All of these activities al-Banna (and others since) subsumed under the Qur'anic term *da'wa*. Sometimes translated as "missionary work," da'wa refers to the original "call" to Islam made by Muhammad and which he commanded his followers to take up as their duty to the world. Al-Banna, however, directed his call not to unbelievers, but to Muslims themselves, calling them back to the true Islam, to transforming themselves into true believers, and to making their society into a true Islamic state.

The other side to da'wa was jihad, al-Banna's second contribution to Islamic thought in the twentieth century. Wahhab had directed his fighting against Muslim "heretics," not the infidels, but now al-Banna argued that once enough faithful Muslims had risen through the call to true Islam, they would again take up their just war with the unbelievers. The first battle would be with the unbelievers who currently occupied Islamic territory. Their repulse was an "individual duty" (*fard 'ayn*), a term from Islamic law that refers to an obligation that falls on every Muslim without exception. While this part of the struggle would begin with Egypt, it would then expand to liberate every piece of Islamic land that was under foreign dominion.[34] Afterward jihad would reach out to include the rest of the world. He argued that

Our task in general is to stand against the flood of modernist civilization overflowing from the swamp of materialistic and sinful desires. This flood has swept the Muslim nation away from the Prophet's leadership and Qur'anic guidance and deprived the world of its guiding light. Western secularism moved into a Muslim world already estranged from its Qur'anic roots, and delayed its advancement for centuries, and will continue to do so until we drive it from our lands. Moreover, we will not stop at this point, but will pursue this evil force to its own lands, invade its Western heartland, and struggle to overcome it until all the world shouts by the name of the Prophet and the teachings of Islam spread throughout the world. Only then will Muslims achieve their fundamental goal, and there will be no more "persecution" and all religion will be exclusively for Allah.[35]

He believed that this task would be an easy one, because European civilization was rotten to its core and failing already. In a passage strangely reminiscent of communist and fascist discourse of the same time, he wrote that "after having sown injustice, servitude and tyranny, [the West] is bewildered, and writhes in its contradictions." Thus, "all that is necessary is for a powerful Eastern hand to reach out, in the shadow of the standard of God on which will float the pennant of the Koran, a standard held up by the army of the faith, powerful and solid; and the world under the banner of Islam will again find calm and peace."[36]

Al-Banna argued that the eventual resort to violence would not be to avenge wrongs suffered, nor to kill the unbelievers, but to save humankind from its many problems. The Qur'an had appointed Muslims as guardians over humanity and given them the right to dominion over the world, but only so that they could guide people to the truth, lead mankind to the good, and illuminate the whole world with the "sun of Islam."[37] Jihad was then a social duty God had delegated to Muslims so that they would become an "army of salvation" to rescue humanity and lead them all together on one path.[38]

Al-Banna's other innovation was to create in 1928 an ideological party, the Muslim Brotherhood (al-Ikhwan al-Muslimin), to carry out his plans. This was superficially a modern, secular solution to the problem, but the Brotherhood was a party that conformed to the Islamic texts and Islamic norms. There are several verses in the Qur'an that talk about "groups," "factions," "sects," and even the "party of God" (Hizbu'llah), and it was these that gave the Brotherhood, and other groups or parties created since then, their theological justification. The Brotherhood was as well a cross-national party, one meant to include all Muslim (men) anywhere, rather than confined to just one country. In addition, the Brotherhood purposely did not engage in Egypt's political life, but instead spent its time occupied in da'wa and the creation of a base of true Muslims. The establishment of social institutions like medical clinics, Islamic banks, social clubs, sport clubs, and religious schools were its main contributions both to the life of the Muslim umma and to its revival.

The ultimately violent aims of al-Banna were not forgotten. In its early years, led by al-Banna, the Brotherhood had a secret armed faction ready to engage in jihad with the British and, once the colonial powers left, with the secular Egyptian governments that replaced them.[39] The Egyptian police killed al-Banna himself after a member of the Brotherhood assassinated the prime minister of Egypt in December 1948. In the face of strong opposition from the government, as well as internal arguments over the killing of Muslims, the Brotherhood would renounce violence during the sixties and repeatedly declare publicly that it would not enter into open warfare. However, various armed groups created by Brotherhood members have sporadically engaged in struggle with governments in Egypt, Syria, Jordan, and elsewhere. An arm of the Brotherhood in Syria revolted against the Ba'athist government twice, in Aleppo (1980) and Hamah (1982). The latter insurrection was brutally crushed by Assad, causing at least ten thousand casualties. After the first Intifada began in 1989, Hamas split off from the Muslim Brotherhood in Palestine and dedicated itself to the liberation of Palestine through violence and the ultimate destruction of Israel. Hamas also continued al-Banna's vision of uniting social transformation with fighting through their support for a full range of social services.[40] Former Brotherhood members who have gone on to create a number of militant groups throughout the Middle East have argued that the current nonviolent message of the Brotherhood is a betrayal of its original, correct strategy, which their group vows to take up and fulfill. Thus, even when not directly involved in violence, the example of the Brotherhood and al-Banna's message of revival, social work, and jihad carried out by an organized Islamic party have influenced the development of many other jihadist and Islamist groups in the Middle East and beyond.

Perhaps the greatest impact that the Brotherhood had was through its most influential member, Sayyid Qutb.[41] Qutb, an Egyptian, began life as a literary critic, open to ideas and influences from the West, but this changed after he traveled to America in the late forties and early fifties. There he experienced racism firsthand and saw the very different social model that Americans offered, especially for the place of women in society.[42] When he returned to Egypt, Qutb joined the Muslim Brotherhood and became increasingly more militant in his views. He also became convinced that his earlier disregard for religion had been wrong: only by a return to "true" Islam would Egypt and the rest of the Islamic world find a way out of its problems and a return to greatness. In 1954, during one of Gamal Abdel Nasser's periodic crackdowns on the Brotherhood, Qutb was arrested and sent to prison. He had been free for only a few months in 1964 when he was rearrested and executed shortly afterward for plotting against the government. It was while he was in prison that Qutb produced his most important works, in particular his exegesis of the Qur'an called *In the Shade of the Qur'an*. The abridged version of this multivolume set, entitled *Milestones* (or *Milestones Along the Way*), became a bestseller in extremist circles and would provide much of the ideological and theological foundation for modern jihadism.

The four most important contributions Qutb made to jihadist thought were a new interpretation of the utter Lordship of God; a fresh understanding of the Islamic term "ignorance" (*jahiliyya*);

an essentialist vision of the world; and his views of jihad. Like Wahhab, Qutb argued that only God has the right to make laws. He concluded from this premise that, first, every element of liberalism was fatally flawed, and second, Muslims had to reject democracy as a false religion, not just as a false political idea. This concept, so central to jihadist ideology, will be discussed in greater detail later. Qutb believed as well that it was the legal system of the state that made it Islamic. Only if the shari'a was used to rule a land was it Islamic, whether the majority of the people in that country called themselves Muslim or not. Qutb asserted that these "so-called Muslims" were still in a state of "ignorance," the expression used by Muhammad to describe the Arabs before they heard the call to Islam. By using this term Qutb was in essence declaring that all Muslims not following Islamic law were unbelievers who could be fought and killed. Qutb argued as well that people's natures did not change over time. In particular, whatever the sacred texts of Islam had to say about the Jews, Christians, and other unbelievers was just as true today as it had always been. As we shall see later, this essentialist conception would allow the creation of conspiracy theories that underlie jihadist views of the West, Christians, Jews, and other unbelievers.[43]

Qutb also supported the idea of jihad, but he envisioned it somewhat differently than either al-Banna or Mawdudi. He believed that Muslims had to engage in a continuous struggle—both armed and intellectual—to eliminate the worship of anyone or anything other than God.[44] Jihad could thus be directed at both unbelievers as well as at any Muslims who refused to recognize the absolute lordship of God. With this re-imagining of jihad, Qutb became an advocate of violence against the "apostate" leaders of Islamic countries—a theme that would reappear in later jihadist discourse and action—as well as a supporter of eternal jihad against all who rejected the call to his vision of "true" Islam.

Although al-Banna was the primary influence on Qutb, the Egyptian theorist was much affected by another contemporary ideologue, Sayyid Abul A'la Mawdudi. Born in British India, Mawdudi, like al-Banna, saw his primary duty as reviving Islam so that Muslims could resist the occupying foreigners. He also believed that Islam was just as threatened by the Hindu majority in India and came to support the two-state solution as the only way to preserve Islam as a community and belief system. Like al-Banna, Mawdudi believed that it would be possible to revive Islam gradually and peacefully through an ideological party, the Jama'at-i-Islami (JI), but he asserted as well that jihad was absolutely essential for the religion and that sooner or later open warfare would come between the believers and the infidels. His followers have since created the equivalent of Hamas, the Hizb-ul-Mujahideen, which wages jihad in Kashmir to free this "Islamic" land from "Hindu" domination. Mawdudi's party, unlike the Muslim Brotherhood, was only rarely involved in violent action (although party members did kill several thousand members of the Ahmadi sect in the fifties) and would eventually turn to political action as the answer, a solution never deemed religiously acceptable by the Muslim Brotherhood. Though eclipsed throughout the eighties and nineties, the JI would make a comeback in 2002 to take power in the North-West Frontier Province as part of the Muttahida Majlis-i-Amal (MMA). Under the MMA, this province, which borders Afghanistan, has adopted Taliban-like laws and provides many of the jihadis now fighting U.S. troops in Afghanistan.

Mawdudi was a prolific writer, and his books, pamphlets, and speeches would broadly influence Islamists and jihadis alike. His belief system, like that of Qutb and al-Banna, began with the proposition that only in Islam would Muslims find the answers to their problems. He too advocated the creation of an Islamic nation governed by the shari'a, a nation that would not separate religion from the rest of life. It was Mawdudi who first revived the term "ignorance," but he used it slightly differently than Qutb did. For him, modernity and liberalism—the entire project of the West—were the contemporary "ignorance" that Muslims had to struggle against and eventually replace with the Islamic system of life. Mawdudi also added a significant piece to jihadist thought as a whole with his interpretation of tawhid, an interpretation shared by Qutb and many other ideologues. Mawdudi argued that because God was one, and sovereign over all of life, nothing was outside the direct control of God and His law. This view of the sovereignty of God (*hakimiyyat Allah*), heralded a form of totalitarianism, with the state and ruler, as God's representatives on earth, delegated to regulate all personal as well as public life. The result of this belief, shared by many jihadis as well as some Islamists, can be seen in places like the Taliban's Afghanistan (the Taliban were also influenced by the JI), Iran, and the Sudan. Perhaps more than al-Banna and Qutb, Mawdudi was affected by the political ideas current at the time, for like the fascists and communists, he too thought the West bankrupt and rotting, about to fade away. He also thought of his party as a vanguard, which in the best Leninist tradition would lead the revolution for the mass of Muslims. He even envisioned the Islamic state that would eventuate be run by a small group of Qur'anically educated and pious clergy, somewhat like the politburo of the Soviet state.[45] Again, it is significant that Mawdudi took these foreign ideas and gave them an Islamic meaning and context, finding ways to justify his prescriptions from the sacred texts.

Together the writings and thought of al-Banna, Qutb, and Mawdudi provided the ideological justifications for later jihadist movements. The important ideas expressed by these three theorists, most especially their views of the new jahiliyya, of tawhid, and of the solution that God has commanded for the believers (jihad), would appear in later statements by groups from Morocco to Indonesia and have provided the rationalization for the declarations of war against the United States, the attacks on the "agent" rulers of most Islamic countries, and the indifference of the jihadis even to the death of Muslim innocents.

3 The Qur'an Is Our Constitution

None of these theorists could have had any impact in the Islamic world if their arguments had not found some sort of resonance in the religion of Islam. More specifically, it could be argued that if Muslims had been confronted by a system of beliefs that had absolutely no foundation in earlier interpretations of their religion, or was not somehow based on the sacred texts that form the bedrock of Islam, they would not have gained a hearing. One reason that al-Banna, Mawdudi, and Qutb would win over followers was their shrewd use of the Qur'an and hadith—as well as the traditional interpreters of these texts—to support their arguments about the need for jihad. This is not to suggest that the underlying economic, social, and political factors have done nothing to give the jihadis a hearing, but rather to propose that these factors do not answer the question of why Islam (rather than, say, nationalism, socialism, or liberalism) has been accepted by many Muslims as a solution to their economic and political dilemmas. Understanding how the extremist groups interpret, use, and abuse the Qur'an, hadith, and these interpreters is thus vital to any discussion of jihadism. The jihadist use of the sacred books is in turn part of the larger struggle taking place within the umma for the soul of Islam. On the one side are the extremists, who want eternal conflict with the unbelievers to define their community and their future. On the other side are socialists, liberals, moderates, and most traditionalists, who want peaceful accommodation with both nonmembers of their community and modernity as a whole. Both factions appeal to the sacred works, which they say support their ideas; both claim to be the true voice of Islam. Only one will, in the end, succeed in convincing the majority of Muslims of their interpretation of the faith.

Jihadist ideologues assert that Muslims must return to the Qur'an and hadith alone to discover how to revive their community. As we have seen, this was the position taken by al-Wahhab, Rida, al-Banna, Qutb, and Mawdudi, all of whom believed that the divine works were a sufficient resource for creating and governing the Islamic community. For the jihadis of today, the interpretations of modern legal scholars and the clergy are not given as much weight as the words of the texts themselves, especially when the sense is "clear."[1] They also assert that the sacred texts must be taken at their most literal and applied in their entirety. The result will be an entire life—not just political, but also social, cultural, and even personal—that is controlled by these books. Abu Hamza al-Masri, leader of al-Muhajiroun, has written that "the Qur'an for mankind is like a manual for a machine. It tells man what to do, what behavior does and does not meet divine approval, and how salvation may be obtained."[2] This is not to say that the jihadis ignore the interpretations of all Islamic scholars; it has just made them extremely selective about which jurisprudents they will listen to. The extremists generally say that they will follow only the Salaf,[3] who collected the hadith and created the science of Islamic jurisprudence (fiqh), laying the basis for the body of law known as the shari'a, and any "righteous" followers of the Salaf.[4] They thus arrogate to themselves the right to pick and choose which authorities they will listen to, as well as the right to interpret and apply the sacred texts for themselves whenever convenient.

While non-Muslims are generally aware of the Qur'an and what it says, they might have trouble understanding how the book could be used as a blueprint for revolutionary action. There are certainly verses that call for struggle against the infidels. The two most often quoted by the jihadis are, "Fight against those who believe not in God, nor in the Last Day, nor forbid that which has been forbidden by God and His Messenger and those who acknowledge not the religion of truth among the people of the Scripture [Jews and Christians], until they pay tribute [*jizya*] with willing submission and feel themselves subdued"; and "Fight them until there is no more dissension and all worship is for God alone."[5] But there are also verses that command Muslims to respect Christians and Jews as fellow believers. Two verses of the Qur'an in particular say that "there is no compulsion in religion" and that every community (even polytheists) has a right to its own beliefs: "To you be your religion, and to me my religion."[6] There is a traditionally accepted Islamic explanation for the two differing messages. The Qur'an was not revealed at one time, but rather gradually, over the course of twenty years, it was "sent down" to fit changing circumstances in the life of the new community. Passages that seem to an outsider to contradict each other are explained by a verse on "abrogation" (*naskh*): later revelation can change or even nullify earlier revelation.[7] Traditional Islamic exegesis of the Qur'an (*tafsir*) is based on the belief that when Muhammad first began to call people to Islam, he was in Mecca, a city that did not welcome his message. It was here that the verses speaking of commonalities with Jews and Christians were revealed. Later, after the migration (*hijra*) to Madinah, he was allowed to call for armed struggle with both polytheists and the "people of the book." Jihadis cite abrogation to claim that these later verses completely negate those that came before. There is thus no longer any need to accept Christians and Jews as fellow believers. They have only the choices outlined in the later verses of the Qur'an—either to accept Islam, to submit to Muslim domination, or to die. Polytheists (like Hindus) have only the choice of conversion or death.

The hadith are less well known than the Qur'an, but anyone

interested in jihadist thought should give them close attention.[8] While Muhammad was alive his followers watched how he lived out the new belief system and reported what they witnessed to the next generation, who in turn relayed this information to the next generation, and so on. Respected scholars among the Salaf brought together the reports of his life and words and arranged them in six collections, each of which is seen as canonical and sacred by (Sunni) Muslims today (the Shi'a have their own collection).[9] The hadith provide the context and explanation of much that is unclear from the Qur'an: how one becomes a Muslim, how prayer is performed, what one must do on the Hajj, and other details of the Islamic life. Non-Muslims may be confused because the Qur'an does not say women must be veiled or that men need to have beards, but the hadith do talk about this—and much more. Even minor particulars of appearance, everyday behavior, and divine worship are covered by the hadith and, for those who take them seriously, are seen as significant. Each of the hadith collections also contain sections (some entire books) on jihad, relations with nonbelievers, and the basic form that an Islamic government should take. Some of these rules can be quite specific. The hadith offer, for instance, laws on acceptable tactics, on the treatment of noncombatants and prisoners of war, and on the need for, and rewards of, jihad. To follow the rules in the hadith is to proclaim one's allegiance to the pious life. This is one of the ways that jihadis are seeking to win their argument against the moderates and liberals who desire peace.

Ayman Zawahri's red-dyed beard, 'Usama bin Ladin's discussion of dreams and their meanings, the jihadis' clothing, the fact that they have given up rich and comfortable lives, all demonstrate their piety to the Islamic world and say that the rest of their (violent) actions should also be understood as part of their righteous lives.

During 1,400 years of interpretive work, Islamic scholars have found other ways to understand the militant and intolerant sections of the Qur'an and hadith. In particular, legists have called into question the concept of "abrogation" since it implies that parts of the sacred texts are no longer valid and that Muslims can therefore ignore them. If the entire Qur'an is the very word of God sent down from an unchanging and perfect book in the heavens (as Islamic dogma affirms), how can whole sections of the infallible word be declared void? The applicability of the militant sections of the Qur'an and hadith to current situations is also problematic, according to some scholars, who ask why only the peaceful and tolerant revelations have been abrogated.[10] Then there is the fact that traditional jurisprudence never accepted all hadith as equally valid, but rather assigned varying degrees of reliability and five different levels of legal responsibility to them (from commands that are obligatory to recommended, to permissible, to reprehensible, to forbidden). Taking these factors into consideration, Khaled Abou El Fadl, one of the foremost Islamic legal scholars, argues that while the Qur'an and other Islamic sources offer the possibility of intolerant interpretations, it does not command them. The fact that Islamic civilizations have been able, throughout the long history of Islam, to find and implement tolerant readings of the texts also offers hope that they can do so in the future.[11] The jihadis have their own answers to these objections, arguing that it is the "true" Muslims (like themselves) who recognize and obey the entire Qur'an and hadith while the liberals and moderates pick and choose which texts they will consider authentic. It is fair to say, then, that it is too early to tell whether the liberal interpretations of the texts will win out, since they are associated with modernist scholars (like Abou El Fadl) who find themselves attacked by the extremists as heretics.

The assertion of the Qur'an and hadith as definitive statements of God's will for mankind has important implications for jihadist views. Because the sacred texts are unchanging—and unchangeable—Islam, the shari'a, and, by extension, jihadist ideology, can never be altered. The tenets of the ideology, based on the Qur'an and hadith, are the very thoughts of God sent down to mankind and are the givens on which humanity must base every action to create a moral and just society. More than that the Qur'an is, unlike the other scriptures given to Christians and Jews, infallible and complete. Traditional Islamic belief is that Christians and Jews deliberately tampered with the Torah and Gospels, altering their message to fit with the sinful desires of the "people of the book." The Qur'an, in contrast, is a perfect copy of God's revelation; nothing can be added to it and nothing can be taken from it. Along with the hadith—the Qur'an says several times that Muhammad is a good example for the believers—humanity has everything it needs to organize existence on earth. That Muhammad was the last prophet means as well that there will be no more divine revelation to alter or adapt Islam to fit in the modern world. It is, rather, the world that must be changed to reflect the truth of Islam. Mankind is not allowed to question the Qur'an, use reason to determine its validity, or to pass judgment upon it.[12] Again, in its scope the Qur'an is universal. Islamic jurists believe that the Torah and Gospels were sent down for a particular people at a particular time, while the Qur'an is for all of humanity throughout all of time. Jihadist ideologues use this generally accepted belief to argue that their interpretation of Islam is also intended for the entire world, which must be brought to recognize this fact peacefully if possible and through violence if not.

The concept of universality has other important implications as well. In jihadist discourse this fact means that within the Qur'an are the secrets of the future as well as the past, and that its pages hold the knowledge necessary to understand the plans and intentions of the Muslims' enemies. Thus a jihadist writer could assert that "Muslims are not required to make political analysis of what the [unbelievers] desire of the Muslims by reading their newspapers or watching what they say on television. Rather Allah . . . has favored the Muslims with Islam which informs us, through the Qur'an, about all their plans. To avoid being shortsighted we must therefore take advantage of this unique window into the unseen to expose their plans and in order to give us a better vision for the future."[13] A jihadist shaikh, discussing the American reaction to September 11, especially the war in Afghanistan and reports that the U.S. government was considering an attack on Arabia, said in an interview, "Many analysts and observers inside and outside America were astonished by the ridiculous justifications and the U.S. violation of value and ethics and by falling in endless contradictions and by violating all international conventions. However one group of observers was actually not surprised. This is the group of Islamic thinkers that examine the world affairs and the international developments and events in light of the Holy Qur'an. . . . Fourteen centuries ago, Allah Most Great, revealed what is in their hearts and warned us from becoming allies with them and He assigned us to call them to the path of Allah and to perform Jihad against them and not to take them as intimate friends and allies."[14]

The universality of the texts explains too the jihadist conviction that the stories, individuals, and nations described in the Qur'an are archetypes that express eternal truths about the nature of good and evil.[15] The Qur'an has numerous recurring narratives about Abraham, Moses, and the other prophets, many of them demonstrating the clash between the righteous and sinners, and the ultimate victory of God's people over evil. The jihadis agree with traditional interpreters that the stories should instruct the umma morally, but add that they are also calling present day Muslims to take action just as the righteous did in the past. And, since the stories have true predictive power, they foretell the victory of the umma and the final defeat of the unbelievers by showing that good has always triumphed over evil. Thus Khomeini asserted that the Qur'an repeats the story of Moses and his confrontation with the Egyptian ruler so frequently because it is telling Muslims today that they need to act as Moses did toward the "Pharaoh of our age," the tyrannical Shah of Iran.[16] This is a quite common comparison—Anwar Sadat was also called Pharaoh, and jihadis see the United States as the newest Pharaoh that must meet its downfall at the hands of the Muslims, as infallible scripture predicts.[17] Bin Ladin and other al-Qaida leaders often refer to specific narrations in the Qur'an and hadith to show that history is repeating itself—the enemies that the true believers faced in the past have returned in new guises to take up the ancient battle of good against evil.[18] Two specific archetypes reiterated by numerous jihadist groups are the Battle of Badr (the first victory of Muhammad and the Muslims over the unbelievers) and the Battle of the Trench (a defensive battle in which the greatly outnumbered small band of Muslims held out against their enemies).[19] Both battles promise victory to the Muslims if they have faith in God, persevere through hardship and persecution, and fight the unbelievers even if outnumbered.

Undoubtedly the most important archetypes from the texts are the Jews and the unbelievers, called by jihadis "the eternal enemies of Islam."[20] They argue that the only guide for interaction between Muslims and the unbelievers must be the Qur'an and hadith, which show the natural conflict between the two.[21] As one jihadist leader writes, there is no reason for this enmity except the fundamental character of these groups: "The simple understanding of the difference between the unbelievers and believers is similar to the difference of light and darkness, black and white or happiness and sadness. It is in the nature of the unbeliever to hate Islam and Muslims. They will do their utmost and their sole aim of living is to destroy or cause harm to the Muslims. This is why the unbelievers have always been fighting against the Muslims and will carry on doing so."[22] This essentialist view of the enemies of Islam means that their depiction in the Qur'an and hadith is valid today in every detail. The Jews in particular have specific negative characteristics, described in the Qur'an and hadith, which still fit them today: they are notorious for their betrayal and treachery; they have incurred God's curse and wrath; they were changed into monkeys and pigs.[23] Qutb was one of the most vehement supporters of this view of the Jews, arguing repeatedly that the interactions of Jewish tribes with Muhammad reflect "the true nature of the Jewish psyche and attitude. These features have accompanied the Jews in every generation and remain typical of their behavior even today. For this reason, the Qur'an has adopted a unique and revealing style in addressing all Israelite generations as one and same, which again makes these accounts relevant for all time:

past, present and future. Thus, the Qur'an's words shall remain a timely and pertinent guide, and a warning, to Muslims in every generation with respect to the identity and potential intrigues of the enemies of their faith."[24]

For jihadis (as well as most Islamists), the Qur'an and hadith have implications, too, for the political life of the Islamic community. The extremist groups assert that the state they create will base its legal system, governing bodies, and foreign policy on the sacred texts alone. "The Qur'an is our constitution," is a well-known slogan, first articulated by Hasan al-Banna and supported today by Islamists and jihadis from Khomeini to Hamas.[25] What exactly this means is also debated by every one of these groups. The jihadist interpretation is that they will reject any system of laws not based on these texts, particularly democracy, which is the ultimate expression of idolatry.[26] They also state that the future leader of the Islamic state will be selected only in ways authorized by the Qur'an and hadith and that the new state will conduct a foreign policy of perpetual jihad because their interpretation of the sacred texts compels it.[27]

Jihadis believe that even the particulars of the eternal jihad are precisely spelled out in the Qur'an and hadith. These details will be described later in some depth; what is important for this part of the discussion is that any action associated with jihad—when to fight, how to fight, what sort of treaties to conclude with the enemy—must find some support from the texts. The essays, manifestos, proclamations, and speeches of jihadis on the issue of fighting the unbelievers thus always return to the sacred writings to justify their interpretation of this holy duty.[28]

Yet the discussion of Qur'anic verses and hadith on jihad, more than on any other topic, shows the willingness of the jihadis to pick and choose which texts they will and will not accept as valid for Muslims today.[29] The emphasis is always on those parts of the books that define jihad as fighting and that paint the relationship between believer and unbeliever in the bleakest terms. Jihadis never mention the texts that talk about tolerance or peace and have declared invalid an important hadith that calls the internal struggle to follow God the "greater jihad" and fighting the "lesser jihad." Perhaps just as importantly, they never give full interpretive weight to the fact that every text was revealed in a set of specific circumstances in the past. Traditionally scholars used these "occasions of revelation" (*asbab al-nuzul*) to inform legal rulings based on analogy, but the jihadis play fast and loose with the strict rules that governed analogy, in effect pulling the specifics of the life of Muhammad out of their historical setting to justify whatever actions they wish.[30]

The jihadist abuse of the holy texts is one of the most important aspects of the current conflict, for the struggle over who controls the Qur'an and hadith is, in many ways, the key to the upheaval in the Islamic world. The jihadis, and their intellectual supporters from among the Islamists, accept only the most literal readings of the sacred texts and the most medieval of the Islamic exegetes. All other readings are not just mistaken, they are pernicious and sinful and must be stamped out. Liberal and moderate Muslims are, on the other hand, open to alternative interpretations of the texts that will allow their community to make peace with modernity and coexist with the rest of mankind. The struggle over the Qur'an and hadith affects both groups' visions of democracy, liberalism, capitalism, international institutions, the rights of women and religious minorities, and jihad. If the extremists win their fight over the Qur'an, their view of democracy, liberals, and capitalism as evil; their belief that international institutions (including the UN) are centers of a conspiracy aimed at destroying Islam; and their medieval notions of the social position of women and minorities—all will come to dominate the Islamic world.

Fortunately, the jihadist assertion of piety and religiously correct behavior has not been uncontested. Some of the most cogent criticisms of jihadist thought and action have come from within the traditional jurists, who have trained for years in the complex rules of interpretation (such as naskh and asbab al-nuzul) and who see the jihadis as heterodox if not outright heretics. As they have pointed out, the extremists have ignored moderate voices among the traditional interpreters of the texts—men like al-Ghazzali and Ibn Khaldun—while giving credence only to those such as Ibn Taymiyya who support their own views. For many Muslims who take their religion seriously, the willingness of the jihadis to selectively ignore a thousand years of interpretive work and the traditional exegesis of the people of knowledge is a serious affront to their understanding of Islam. The struggle over the Qur'an and hadith, like the battles by moderates against extremists taking place in many Islamic countries, is still in process, with the final result far from clear. There is hope, however, that a more tolerant vision of orthodox Islam can win out, using the very traditions and texts that the extremists claim to honor.

4 Our 'Aqida

When the reality contradicts with Islam, it is not allowed to
interpret Islam so as to agree with reality, because this would be a
distortion of Islam; instead the duty requires changing the reality
so as to conform to Islam.

—Hizb al-Tahrir

With the Qur'an and the hadith as their only sources, the various
jihadist groups believe they have all they need to discover the
comprehensive ideology that Islam contains. And jihadis see that
as their duty. They sincerely believe that as Islam has demands
on all of life, it also has the answers for all of life. Their goal is to
discover what these answers are through the sacred texts alone
and then to link them into a coherent and all-embracing worldview. The three most important ideologues of the movement, al-
Banna, Mawdudi, and Qutb, provided the intellectual groundwork and the basic foundations for this ideology, and later work
by lesser known jihadis filled in the gaps, so that there would be
none of life left out. On this point the two terms that the extremists use for ideology is telling. The first, 'aqida, generally trans-
lates as "[religious] creed," but the jihadis have reinterpreted and

broadened it to mean any political or religious doctrine.[1] Unlike Western ideologies—political by definition—the jihadis want their 'aqida to speak to every aspect of human existence, the personal as well as the social. Qutb was not the first or the last to write that "Islam has a mandate to order the whole of human life."[2] In even stronger language, Qutb called the Western idea of separation between religion and the rest of life the "hideous schizophrenia" that would lead to the downfall of "white civilization" and its replacement by Islam. Religion, he wrote, "can be but dominant master: powerful, dictating, honored and respected; ruling, not ruled, leading, not led."[3] The other term sometimes used for ideology—*nizam* (system)—is just as expansive, including within its scope the economic, political, cultural, and personal spheres of human life.[4] For jihadis, the distinction between religious and political, private and public, disappears, replaced by a vision of life unified into one whole.[5]

The basic principle of jihadist ideology—the absolute unity of God—reflects this belief. Technically know as tawhid, it is the first tenet of Islam, for everyone who becomes a Muslim must state publicly and believe privately that "there is no divinity but God, and Muhammad is the prophet of God." This declaration, known as the *shahada*, forms the basis for Islamic thinking about true religion: there is only one God who has no partners or equals. Jihadis have redefined this central belief and given it an all-embracing significance. Sayyid Qutb was again best at articulating what tawhid meant for the extremists, writing that "Islam is the religion of unity among all the forces of the universe, so it is inescapably the religion of tawhid, it recognizes the unity of God, the unity of all the religions in the religion of God, and the unity of the Apostles in preaching this one religion since the dawn of life. Islam is the religion of unity between worship and social relations, creed and Shari'a, spiritual and material things, economic and spiritual values, this world and the afterlife, and earth and heaven. From this great unity issue its laws and commands, its moral directives and restrictions, and its precepts for the conduct of government and finance, for the distribution of income and losses, and for [determining] rights and duties. In that great principle are included all the particulars and details."[6] Tawhid is thus transformed from a statement about the nature of God into a description of the unity of the entire universe and the unity of all man's activities within that universe.

The principle of tawhid has three significant implications for the political/religious ideology of the jihadis, two initially formulated by Mawdudi and the last proposed by Qutb. The first comes directly from the Qur'anic argument that God, unique and without partners, is the only being who deserves worship. If this is true, humanity needs to recognize Him as sole master and ruler, argued Mawdudi, and to see themselves as the slaves of God bound by their very nature to obey Him. He pointed out that the word used for "worship" in Islam—*ibada*—is related to the term for "slave" (*'abd*) and that "'ibada does not merely mean ritual or any specific form of prayer. It means a life of continuous service and unremitting obedience like the life of a slave in relation to his Lord."[7] But, Mawdudi added, because some men like to play at being gods while others like to recognize men as their lords, this proper relationship between humanity and the divine has been overturned and replaced by the domination of man by man. The consequences of this perversion were severe and far-reaching: tyranny, despotism, intemperance, unlawful exploitation, and inequality. Mawdudi in fact believed that "*the root-cause of all evil and mischief* in the world is *the domination of man over man*, be it direct or indirect."[8] Thus "Islam's call for the affirmation of faith in one God and offering devotion to Him alone was an invitation to join a movement of social revolution." Mawdudi then offered a class analysis to show that the people who would benefit most from Islam were precisely those oppressed groups targeted by socialist and communist rhetoric.[9] His use of contemporary terminology is, of course, deliberate, meant to preempt socialist appeals to Muslims and to show that Islam was concerned about social justice long before Marx.

The second implication of tawhid follows directly from the first. If only God is to be worshipped and obeyed, then only His laws have any significance. This was the point that Ibn Taymiyya had made eight hundred years ago, now revived by Mawdudi, Qutb, and the rest of the jihadis and made into their most important critique of the Islamic world and the West. The basic principle of Islam, Mawdudi would write, means that "human beings must, individually and collectively, surrender all rights of overlordship, legislation and exercising of authority over others. No one should be allowed to pass orders or make commands *on his own right* and no one ought to accept the obligation to carry out such commands and obey such orders."[10] In legal/political terms this formulation of tawhid (specifically named *tawhid al-rububiyya* [the lordship of God] or hakimiyyat Allah [God's rule]) means that only God has sovereignty. The people (as envisaged in most democracies), rulers, legislatures, and even entire nations have no inherent sovereignty or right to rule—to God alone belongs this exclusive right.[11] The only role left for a nation's "leaders" is to implement God's laws, not to modify in any way the least of his commands.

Sayyid Qutb agreed with Mawdudi that God's sovereignty was key to understanding Islam and the political life of the Islamic nation. His argument would, however, lead to a different perspective of the implications of tawhid and produce revolutionary conclusions about Islam, the nature of the modern world, and the mission of the believers. Qutb began by arguing that servitude to God meant true freedom for humanity.

This religion is really a universal declaration of the freedom of man from servitude to other men and from servitude to his own desires, which is also a form of human servitude; it is a declaration that sovereignty belongs to God alone and that He is the Lord of all the worlds. It means a challenge to all kinds and forms of systems which are based on the concept of the sovereignty of man; in other words, where man has usurped the Divine attribute. Any system in which the final decisions are referred to human beings, and in which the sources of all authority are human, deifies human beings by designating others than God as lords over men. This declaration means that the usurped authority of God be returned to Him and the usurpers be thrown out—those who by themselves devise laws for others to follow, thus elevating themselves to the status of lords and reducing others to the status of slaves. In short, to proclaim the authority and sovereignty of God means to eliminate all human kingship and to announce the rule of the Sustainer of the universe over the entire earth.[12]

The objective of Islam is thus to declare humanity's freedom both philosophically and in actual life.[13] In this interpretation of tawhid, Islam becomes a sort of liberation theology, designed to end oppression by human institutions and man-made laws and to return God to his rightful place as unconditional ruler of the world.

For Qutb then—as for Mawdudi—it was vitally important that God's sovereignty was absolute. The result would be a revolution in human understanding of who deserves power and authority. As he pointed out, even the Arabs of Muhammad's time realized that "ascribing sovereignty only to God meant that the authority would be taken away from the priests, the leaders of tribes, the wealthy and the rulers, and would revert to God. It meant that only God's authority would prevail in the heart and conscience, in matters pertaining to religious observances and in the affairs of life such as business, the distribution of wealth and the dispensation of justice—in short, in the souls and bodies of men."[14] But this was not enough for Qutb. In order to fulfill the true meaning of tawhid, he argued that God's sovereignty also had to be absolutely recognized and realized. On a personal level, this analysis transformed the definition of who was a true Muslim. Traditionally, parentage or a public declaration was enough to establish who was or who was not a Muslim. Qutb insisted that this was not enough, writing that a Muslim had to put God's laws into practice or he was not, according to the shari'a, a Muslim at all.[15] To be a real Muslim, he wrote, was "to believe in [God] in one's heart, to worship Him Alone, *and to put into practice His laws.* Without this complete acceptance of 'La ilaha illa Allah,' which differentiates the one who says he is a Muslim from a non-Muslim, there cannot be any practical significance to this utterance, nor will it have any weight according to Islamic law."[16] This was because "obedience to laws and judgments [other than God's] is a sort of worship, and anyone who does this is considered out of this religion. It is taking some men as lords over others, while this religion has come to annihilate such practices, and it declares that all the people of the earth should become free of servitude to anyone other than God."[17] It was this revolutionary conclusion that would allow some later jihadis to declare *takfir* on (declare as unbelievers) most of the Islamic world.[18] This is significant, because declaring takfir gave these groups the necessary legal justification to fight and kill—as they would unbelievers—any Muslims who did not agree with their vision of Islam.

On a political level, Qutb's analysis of tawhid led him to conclude that Islam could not exist as a creed in the heart alone, but had to have power and a state that implemented Islamic law fully. Yet because there were no longer any lands based on the shari'a in this way, he argued that Islam did not exist anywhere in the world.[19] For Muslims, this statement was both shocking and divisive. Indeed, it is not too much to assert that the divide between jihadis and the rest of the Islamic world runs through this radical claim. Most Muslims refused to believe that Islam had simply disappeared and therefore did not accept the rest of Qutb's analysis about what had to be done to change this dire situation. For those who did agree that authentic Islam had vanished, it was not difficult to go along with Qutb's next step: a call on Muslims to "restore" God's sovereignty by violently seizing power and setting up a "real" Islamic state. It is also significant that Qutb envisaged this Islamic state in the same totalizing terms as Mawdudi. In fact, he argued that *the* distinguishing feature of the new country would be its dedication to implementing every command, rule, and law of the shari'a, obeying God and Muhammad completely. The people of the authentic Islamic state would also be "true" Muslims who would "devote their entire lives in submission to God," would never decide any affair on their own but instead would "refer to God's injunctions concerning it and follow them."[20] The state would have to become involved in this process, because "legislation is not limited only to legal matters, as some people assign this narrow meaning to the shari'a. The fact is that attitudes, the way of living, the values, criteria, habits and traditions, are all legislated and affect people."[21]

What, then, about the nations that called themselves Islamic? What were they if not Muslim? It is here that Qutb proposed a radical concept that would again deeply influence later jihadist groups. He argued that there were only two kinds of societies: Islamic and *jahili*. The term *jahili* is taken from the earliest days of Islam and is the adjective for the word *jahiliyya*, (ignorance), which Muhammad used to refer to the state of the Arab world before he brought the message of Islam. Although jahili literally means "ignorant," a better translation is probably "pagan," since it has that general sense of benighted unbelief about it. Qutb redefined jahiliyya, arguing that in current circumstances it was no longer that "simple and primitive" ignorance of the ancient world, but rather had taken the form "of claiming that the right to create values, to legislate rules of collective behavior, and to choose any way of life rests with men, without regard to what God has prescribed." Modern versions of jahiliyya were thus political/economic systems like communism and capitalism, man-made concepts that had created the oppression, humiliation, and exploitation devastating the entire earth.[22] This line of reasoning had far-reaching implications. If, as Qutb argued, there were no truly Islamic societies in existence, then every country in the world was jahili. The only conclusion that Muslims could draw from this statement was that even those nations that called themselves Islamic were pagan and therefore, according to Islamic law, illegitimate.[23] As we shall see, with this declaration, in conjunction with his assertion that most of the planet's Muslims could be pronounced unbelievers and killed, Qutb was justifying outright warfare on the entire Islamic world.

The third implication of tawhid is ostensibly religious in nature but has political implications. Jihadis argue that since God is one, his religion, in turn, must be one. They conclude from this that not only is Islam the only form of worship acceptable to God, but that other religions are positive evils. For Qutb, Islam was "pure, just, beautiful, springing from the source of the Most High, the Most Great God," and could not mix at all with the "filth" of jahiliyya, within which he included all the "man-made" religions of the world. A common synonym for Islam in jihadist discourse is *al-Haqq*,—the Truth—while all other religions, philosophies, and belief systems are batil,—falsehood.[24] There can be no mixing of the two and no equating of them: one is absolutely right and good, all others are absolutely wrong and evil. The language that is used to describe Islam emphasizes its purity versus the uncleanness, impurity, and corruption of all other religions. As we shall see, an emphasis on the oneness of religion would allow jihadis to fight against not only polytheists (like Hindus), but also the traditionally tolerated communities of Jews and Christians. Of course, from a purely Islamic viewpoint this conclusion has two serious problems. First, while a few scholars have agreed with it, there are widely respected branches of fiqh and the shari'a that do not. It is also important that this conclusion has no satisfying explanation for Muhammad's tolerance of other religions. After all, if they are all false, distorted versions of the true religion—and the people who practice them are rejecters of the true faith—why should they be allowed to live at all, let alone have a protected position in the Islamic state?

The philosophical groundwork by Mawdudi and Qutb on tawhid—as well as the earlier work by Wahhab and even Ibn Taymiyya—have numerous echoes in the writings and statements of jihadis today.[25] Shaikh 'Abd ul-Qadir bin 'Abd ul-Aziz, an Egyptian associated with Jund al-Islam (a jihadist group fighting in northern Iraq) and with 'Usama bin Ladin, uses Ibn Taymiyya's work to argue that anyone who rules with other than the Qur'an and hadith is an unbeliever, and any state ruled in this way is an unbelieving state that must be opposed.[26] The Muslim Unification Council, founded in 1999 as part of a global jihad network to work on "re-unifying the Muslim umma into one super state," declared in its basic policy statement that "sovereignty belongs to Allah . . . not the Moslem's! [*sic*] . . . All Governments (adopting western democracy and/or members of the UN) in Muslim Land must be removed immediately. . . . Organizations such as the UN, IMF and World Bank are enemies to ISLAM and must be classified as enemy organizations."[27] A Canadian jihadi argued in an Australian jihadist magazine that "there can be absolutely nothing legislated other than the shari'a of Islam. And there can be no governing except by what Allah has revealed. . . . Whoever has put his own laws, instead of the shari'a, into the governing of man; they are committing *shirk* [polytheism] and Kufr [unbelief] and have left Islam. . . . The rulers who have done this are the leaders of Kufr. They are at war with Allah and must be fought and killed until all *din* [religion] is for Allah alone."[28] The jihadist group Hizb al-Tahrir, now linked by several governments to al-Qaida, uses much of the space in its publications arguing the same points: that there can be no separation between religion and politics; that any state that fails to apply the entire shari'a is kufr and must be destroyed; and that "true" Muslims are those who understand tawhid only in this way.[29] Fathi Yakan, one of the heads of the Syrian Muslim Brotherhood—a much more radical and violent variety of the Brotherhood than the Egyptian version—touches on every one of the themes outlined by Mawdudi and Qutb. He argues in his seminal work, *To Be a Muslim*, that the shahada means God alone is divine and sovereign and therefore

Islamic teachings and rules are comprehensive and designed by Allah to govern the affairs of man at all levels of community, from the family to the whole of the human race. . . . Islam alone can provide the power for Muslims to liberate oppressed peoples from the control of those who worship the false gods of modernist and postmodernist cultures. . . . The adoption and adaptation of capitalist, socialist, communist or other manmade systems, either in whole or in part, constitutes a denial of Islam and disbelief in Allah the Lord of the worlds. . . . Muslims in an Islamic Movement are the true servants of Allah and their obedience is only to Allah, the Almighty, in all matters of life. It encompasses not only religious affairs but also worldly affairs. This is because Islam teaches its followers that there is no segregation or separation between religion and worldly affairs. . . . The servitude of man means that he must reject all manmade philosophies and systems that by nature lead mankind to submit to the false gods of materialism.[30]

The Canadian Institute of Contemporary Islamic Thought not only supports the usual Qutbist analyses of tawhid, but also agrees that the United States and the West are the modern jahiliyya.[31] Then there is Abu Hamza al-Masri, an Egyptian jihadist cleric accused by the British government of supporting terrorism. In his writing, speeches, and sermons, Abu Hamza has reinterpreted Qur'anic verses to show that absence of the shari'a is the same as polytheism.[32] He agrees with Qutb that ruling by other than God's laws is more than just a minor sin, but rather one that takes a Muslim out of the religion, thus declaring takfir on at least the rulers of the entire Islamic law, and even uses the Qutbian term *hakimiyya* to talk about the importance of tawhid for the political world of the "true" Muslims.[33]

Finally, 'Usama bin Ladin's first public stance was against the un-Islamic political, diplomatic, and economic policies of King Fahd—and in particular the Saudi ruler's support for the infidel American forces in the Arabian peninsula. Yet in his lengthy letter to the king rebuking him for his "unbelieving" decisions, bin Ladin referred constantly to the major evil committed by the Saudi government: ruling by other than the laws that God had sent. His preamble to the letter stated that "the quintessence of our dispute is the fact that your ruling system has transgressed 'la ilaha illa Allah,' . . . and that is the basis of Tawhid . . . that differentiates between belief and disbelief. All the aforementioned problems are a result of your transgression against the basic tenants of Tawhid."[34] In his 1996 declaration of war against the United States, generally ignored in the West because it relied on language largely incomprehensible to non-Muslims, bin Ladin listed amongst the Saudi government's crimes "the arbitrary declaration of what is . . . lawful and unlawful regardless of the Shari'a as instituted by Allah," and that they had suspended Islamic law and used man-made law instead. The significance of this for him was that "as stated by the people of knowledge, it is not a secret that to use man-made law instead of the Shari'a and to support the infidels against the Muslims is one of the ten 'voiders'[35] that would strip a person from his Islamic status."[36] In an early interview bin Ladin also agreed with Qutb's understanding of jahiliyya, describing the entire world—including all Islamic states—as still in that state of "ignorance" and "disbelief."[37]

The obvious deduction from the jihadist ideology is that every element of modern Western liberalism is flawed, wrong, and evil. The basis of liberalism (in the eyes of the jihadis) is secularism—the complete separation of religion and state— Qutb's "hideous schizophrenia." Some groups, like Hizb al-Tahrir, see this as part of a compromise between "two contradictory ideas; the idea which the clergy used to call for in the 'Medieval Ages,' namely the submission of everything in this life to the 'Religion,' i.e. Christianity and the idea which some thinkers and philosophers called for, namely the denial of the existence of a Creator." The separation of the two powers gave each its own sphere over which to reign supreme, meaning in reality that religion no longer had any say over life.[38] Other jihadis, including Qutb, argue that this is part and parcel of Christianity, a result of a misreading (or deliberate invention) of Jesus' statement to "give to Caesar what is Caesar's and to God what is God's," but actually motivated by the weaknesses of Christianity in its earliest days and especially its inability to seize and hold state power.[39] Whatever the source of the idea, jihadis argue that it is un-Islamic, a foreign concept introduced by the West to weaken the Muslims and keep them from implementing

Islam to its fullest. Groups like Hamas refuse to work with any party that espouses secularism, while others—including al-Qaida—have been willing to compromise on this principle in order to fight against a mutual enemy.[40]

The separation of religion and state explains for the jihadis why the West (and the United States in particular) have no moral sense: by keeping religion from influencing life, Christians and Jews have in fact destroyed the only source of ethics and morality and therefore have no aim in life but "to seek benefit and enjoyment."[41] In the fullest discussion of this idea, Hizb al-Tahrir argues that because spiritual matters are confined to the religion and clergy, "there are no moral, spiritual or humanitarian values in the Western [civilization], rather only materialistic ones. Owing to this, humanitarian actions became affiliated to organizations separated from the state, such as the Red Cross and the missionaries. Every value, apart from the chief materialistic value of benefit[,] was excluded from life."[42] Qutb recognized that liberalism had values, but believed that they were never fully developed or implemented and "were insufficient for a progressive humanity." With the exhaustion of the ideas expressed in the Magna Carta and the French Revolution—and separated from religion that might have presented eternal values—"white civilization" had become "sterile" and therefore could be seen in retrospect as nothing but a "temporary civilization."[43]

The entire concept of democracy comes in for special condemnation by jihadis. Unlike Islamists, who agree that there should be no separation between religion and politics but who do not necessarily reject democratic governance, jihadis want nothing to do with "man-made" laws or men legislating according to their own choices and desires. Mawdudi again first articulated this point, arguing that Islam was the "very antithesis of secular Western democracy," with its ideas of sovereignty for the people and absolute powers of legislation in the hands of elected officials.[44] Qutb too rejected any human participation in the making of laws—a function that is the sole province of God. In even more vehement terms than Mawdudi, he warned against any attempts to mix the Islamic system—perfect, comprehensive, and completely untouched by error—with human systems like democracy that were none of these things.[45] Jihadis today have made a critique of democracy the centerpiece of their ideology. Hizb al-Tahrir has been particularly passionate in its publication and its work against democracy. The group has argued that adopting Western laws and democratic rules is so evil that even if laws identical to those of the shari'a were legislated, the fact that they were adopted in a democratic system would make them wrong and "kufr."[46] In an article on the evils of democracy, Hizb al-Tahrir compared backing parties that are based on secularism, democracy, socialism, or nationalism (specifically mentioning the "Republican or Democratic parties in America, the Labour or Conservative parties in Britain and the PPP and Muslim League in Pakistan") to supporting prostitution and gambling.[47] 'Umar Bakri Mohammad, a member of the Syrian Muslim Brotherhood and founder of al-Muhajiroun, as well as an outspoken supporter of 'Usama bin Ladin, argues that participating in any way in the democratic process (whether by voting or by actually running for office) is forbidden [*haram*]. The term used is significant because he is claiming to be able to give a religious ruling (fatwa) that should, theoretically, be binding on all Muslims.[48] Efforts by Muslims to locate an Islamic vision of democracy in the concept known as *shura*[49] are met with scorn by the jihadis. The attempt to equate the two concepts "springs from a lack of understanding and self-confidence," a member of the ICIT argues, because they "have little or nothing in common."[50]

International law and governance are likewise rejected by jihadis who view the UN as both a wholly owned subsidiary of the United States and Europe, and as the proponent of a legal system at odds with Islam. The idea of international law is detested for exactly the same reason as democracy: it ignores the shari'a and is based ultimately on the non-Islamic notion that nations can "make up" any laws that they please.[51] In any case, jihadis believe that Westerners created the current international legal system to protect their own rights and not to uphold true (Islamic) justice.[52] One jihadist group traces the origins of international law to the "exclusively Christian" treaty of Westphalia, arguing thus that from its very inception, "International norms were established by Christian powers seeking to further their hegemony and protect their interests."[53] Meanwhile, jihadis argue that the basic purpose of the UN is either to allow the West to maintain control over the world's wealth and resources, or to grant legitimacy to their intervention in the affairs of weak countries—most especially the Islamic world.[54]

Jihadis condemn too the economic views of classical liberalism—one of several points wherein their critique of the West meets the critique of various leftist movements. A caveat is in order, however. As with other words, jihadis have taken the term capitalism and reinterpreted it to fit their own worldview. In Hizb al-Tahrir discourse, as well as in discussions by several other jihadist groups, capitalism means "the separation of religion from the rest of life." A better way to translate the word in many jihadist publications would thus be "secular liberalism," since this is essentially the meaning that it has for them. Even when the word capitalism is used approximately as it would be in the West, jihadis—motivated by their allegiance to the Qur'an and hadith—attack slightly different aspects of the economic system than the Left generally does. One of the central foci for jihadist criticism of capitalism is, for instance, the charging of interest. The Qur'an and Muhammad rejected outright any usury and in fact promised warfare with Arab tribes that continued to charge interest. In his exegesis of the Qur'an, Qutb stated (in rather hyperbolic language) that there is "no other issue [that] has been condemned and denounced so strongly in the Qur'an as usury." Why is it taken so seriously? Because "it is based on the total rejection of God's role and the dismissal of all the principles and aims on which the Divine code of living is founded."[55] He concluded that "wherever usury is adopted as a system the faith of Islam, as a whole, does not exist."[56] One of bin Ladin's earliest criticisms of the Saudis was their decision to allow banks to charge interest on loans, their borrowing of money with interest, and the "sea of debt" in which they had allowed the country to drown. He emphasized the Qur'anic injunction to make war on those who charge interest as well as the fact that anyone "who legislates and passes laws that sanction usury is an apostate disbeliever."[57] His 1996 declaration of war against the United States repeated these charges, again stressing that to charge interest meant war with the "true" believers.[58] Another statement by al-Qaida lists usury as one of the crimes that the United States has committed and ties this to another theme of jihadist thought: that the Jews (through charging interest and other devious means) really control the United States.[59] In a statement issued shortly after the September 11 attacks, a Saudi cleric who has consistently supported bin Ladin rebuked his fellow clerics for daring to condemn an assault on that "center of usury," the World Trade Center.[60] The result of jihadist rejection of this aspect of liberalism is that stock markets, financial markets, Western-style banks, and even paper money (Muhammad used only gold and silver money) are all condemned as evil by jihadis.

Jihadist notions of private property constitute their other major economic criticism of liberalism. According to the jihadis, God is the true owner of all property, and man is allowed to use it only when he does so in an Islamic correct way. Capitalist ideas about ownership are therefore condemned by some jihadis in terms reminiscent of critiques by the Left, but with an Islamic form. Qutb, for instance, believed God's ownership of property meant that "fundamentally property belongs to the community as a whole and private property is a function with conditions and limitations," a definition that many socialists could agree with.[61] A draft constitution for an Islamic state, written by Hizb al-Tahrir, gives a slightly different twist to these views. The constitution forbids companies and cooperatives outright, outlaws the sale to unbelievers of any land "opened up" by jihad (thus making illegal, for instance, the sale of land to Jews in Israel), and mandates state control of all mineral resources and any factories that work with mineral resources.[62] This latter point finds resonance with several jihadist groups and is the basis for their critique of the "squandering" of oil resources by the Saudis and other Arab governments, resources which they believe should be used as a weapon in the struggle with the West either by refusing to sell it at all or at the very least selling it to the unbelievers at far higher prices.[63] In a 2002 statement al-Qaida listed what it said were American crimes that had led to the declaration of war on all Americans. The group accused the United States of stealing "our wealth and oil at paltry prices" through international influence and military threats, committing a theft that was the biggest "ever witnessed by mankind in the history of the world."[64]

The jihadist rejection of personal freedom, the bedrock of liberalism, is perhaps the most difficult aspect of their ideology for Westerners, but it follows directly from their interpretation of tawhid. As noted earlier, Qutb argued strenuously that Islam had come to bring true and universal freedom to the world: a freedom from tyranny and liberation from servitude to other men.[65] At the same time, jihadis deny that people have, or should be granted, the freedom to do whatever they wish because this permits what God has forbidden and would not force people to do what God has commanded. They also argue that there are sound practical reasons for denying people freedom. Mawdudi discussed the natural weaknesses of humanity (drinking, economic ills, political domination by classes, and "that satanic flood of female liberty and license which threatens to destroy human civilization"), all of which showed the need to limit human freedoms.[66] Hizb al-Tahrir (whose name, ironically, means the Liberation Party) has argued that this sort of freedom has turned "capitalist" societies "into jungles of wild animals in which the strong devours the weak and man degenerates to the level of the animal as a result of unleashing his instincts and organic needs." Western notions of freedom are, for the "Liberation Party," nothing but "the freedom of fornication, sexual perversion, immorality, drinking alcohol, and other diseases."[67] More broadly, jihadis reject the concept of human rights, which emanates from this central idea of freedom, as a contradiction of Islam. An article by al-Muhajiroun, an offshoot of Hizb al-Tahrir, condemns every part of the UN's Universal Declaration of Human Rights, and especially Article 3 ("Everyone has the right to life, liberty and security of person") because "Liberty is just another name for freedom, the profane idea used to impose the disease of secularism world-wide."[68] 'Umar Bakri Mohammad explicitly links the concepts of freedom, democracy, capitalism, and secular thought, calling all of them "poison . . . which the fangs of the imperialist [unbelievers] injected in our thinking," and from which the Islamic community is only now beginning to heal.[69] When a jihadist writer declares that "we will enter the White House and destroy the idols of democracy and liberty as the Prophet . . . entered Makkah and destroyed the idols," the opposition between liberalism and jihadism could not be more clear.[70]

Jihadis are equally vehement in their rejection of religious freedoms. As we have seen, their interpretation of tawhid allows the existence of only one true religion: all others are not just false, they are described as wicked perversions of the truth, whose followers must be contained, subdued, and humiliated.[71] The jihadis therefore reject liberal ideals like religious equality, the idea of an "Abrahamic faith" (that would bring together Islam, Judaism, and Christianity) and even mechanisms for improving relations between religions like interfaith dialogue.[72] For historical as well as current political reasons, Judaism, Christianity, and Hinduism are the religions most often discussed and dismissed by the jihadis, but their analysis of these belief systems would fit equally well with any other religion. Qutb's examination of Judaism and Christianity is particularly enlightening. Throughout his exegesis of the Qur'an, he continually emphasizes the treachery, corruption, and absolute falsehood of the Jews and Christians. When he examines verses that talk about the betrayals and evils of these "people of the book," he concludes that the revelations are meant for all time and speak to the eternal qualities of these communities.[73] Yet when he analyzes those verses that talk about toleration or even recognize Jews and Christians as fellow believers, he claims that they speak only to very specific circumstances in Muhammad's ministry and are no longer in effect.[74] Other jihadis have taken up these themes and use them as the centerpiece of their rejection of dialogue, compromise, or even discussion with other religious groups. Abu Hamza, for instance, concludes, "Only the most ignorant and animal minded individuals would insist that prophet killers (Jews) and Jesus worshippers (Christians) deserve the same right as us."[75] This emphasis on the negative qualities of all other religions naturally leads to the conclusion that Islam is superior to other religions or belief systems, and commands Muslims to hate followers of other religions while loving and supporting other Muslims only.[76]

Thus the ideology that forms the basis for the jihadis' actions necessarily implies a complete rejection of all other belief systems—whether the West calls them religions or ideologies—including liberalism. This rejection is more than a simple refusal to accept these belief systems as valid or to acknowledge them at least as equals, but is rather a declaration that they must be destroyed.[77] Despite the many sections of the Qur'an and the hadith that speak to the contrary, they declare that God does not want differing belief systems to coexist: all religion must be for Him alone. The jihadis recognize that the West will not submit without a fight and believe in fact that the Christians, Jews, and liberals have united against Islam in a war that will end in the complete destruction of the unbelievers.

5 The Clash of Civilizations, Part I

THE AMERICAN CAMPAIGN TO SUPPRESS ISLAM

The conflict that jihadis believe is inevitable has nothing to do with Samuel Huntington's "clash of civilizations." Instead it is a fusion of their views of liberalism as the ultimate evil with medieval Islamic theories that divided the world into two hostile factions: the House of Islam and the House of War.[1] The House of Islam (*dar al-Islam*) included all territory under the rule of Islam, while the House of War (*dar al-harb*) was the rest of the world that refused to recognize the authority of Islam and therefore was open to warfare. Unlike most Muslims today, jihadis accept this dichotomous view of the world—it is, in fact, the centerpiece of their foreign policies—although they have made significant changes to the original medieval theory. Most importantly, jihadis rarely talk about the "House of Islam" because few of them believe that true Islam exists anywhere in the world. Instead a majority argue that the fundamental division of the world is between supporters of the Truth (al-Haqq—true Islam) and its eternal enemy, falsehood (batil)—also called "unbelief" (kufr).[2] The two are completely incompatible. When the first messengers were sent to mankind by God to preach the Truth, falsehood immediately arose to oppose it. For jihadis, the struggle between the two principles, which are always embodied by groups of people, is an "inherent part of Allah's creation" and one of the "universal laws of life," laid down in the Qur'an.[3] In fact God ordained a law of enmity between human beings at the beginning of time so that "it is in the nature of the unbeliever to hate Islam and Muslims."[4] 'Umar Bakri Mohammad takes this line of reasoning one step further, arguing that by their very nature all ideologies must expand or contract: there is no middle ground of coexistence or cooperation. Thus Islam must expand to fill the entire world or else falsehood in its many guises will do so.[5]

For some jihadis it is not enough to assert that the conflict is a natural part of God's order. To satisfy their reading of Islamic law, they must find some way to show that the current enemies of Islam are the aggressors, that it is they who have begun the war that continues to this day. The result is three elaborate theories about "unbelief" that are used to blame anyone other than "true" Muslims for the conflict between Islam and liberalism. One theory claims that people or groups mentioned in the Qur'an and hadith—the unbelievers who confronted Muhammad—are the same today as they were fourteen hundred years ago; another that the enemies of Islam represent a concept known as *taghut*, which is often mentioned in the sacred texts; or, if the current enemies cannot have any possible connection to the Qur'anic narratives, a third theory argues that they somehow embody the principle of unbelief (or falsehood). It is worth emphasizing that by taking this interpretive route, these jihadis begin by locating the problems of the Muslim community within the actions of outsiders and do not therefore blame other Muslims as greatly for the economic, political, or social difficulties of the umma. This is an important point, because it has meant that jihadist groups have generally targeted unbelievers rather than ordinary Muslims although, as we shall see, they have found ways to excuse the "incidental" deaths of even innocent Muslims.

The first theory about unbelief is generally the most common, and jihadis who use it ascribe to the concept of "archetypes" discussed earlier. They assert that Jews and Christians, the modern proponents of liberalism, have the very same attributes and goals as the communities Muhammad first clashed with, still desiring especially the destruction of Islam. Qutb, one of the foremost proponents of this view, argued repeatedly throughout his commentary on the Qur'an that the Jews allied themselves with unbelief, began the war with Muhammad, and have continued their deadly struggle to this day.[6] In his reading of the Jews today, they are exactly the same people as they were fourteen centuries ago, allowing Muslims to use the Qur'an and hadith to understand their nature and their strategies and how to defeat them.[7] Other jihadis (and many Islamists) have agreed with Qutb, describing in detail the inherent evil of the Jews and the eternal characteristics that have earned them God's curse.[8] Because of this incompatibility of Islam and the Jews, war with them is, bin Ladin has said, "inevitable."[9]

The jihadis condemn as well the Christians, most of whom rejected Muhammad's message and (in the form of the Byzantine Empire) fought with the nascent Islamic state. A verse from the Qur'an often repeated by the jihadis is "Never will the Jews and Christians be satisfied with you until you leave your religion." Although obviously directed at Muhammad, jihadis have reinterpreted the "you" to mean all Muslims and the "Jews and Christians" to mean Europe and America with their "religion" of liberalism. Invective directed against these "Christians" today resembles that used against the Jews.[10] Another tack is taken by a jihadist argument that modern Christians are controlled by the Jews, who plan to exploit them for the original Jewish goal of destroying Islam.[11]

Qutb believed that the nature of the Jews and Christians, as revealed in the Qur'an and hadith, showed that they were entirely responsible for the struggle between Islam and the unbelievers. He asserted that the "peoples of earlier revelations"[12] knew that Muhammad spoke the truth and that what he recited confirmed their own books.[13] Why then, despite this knowledge, did they choose to side with "falsehood" and "unbelief" and attack him? Qutb argued that there were many reasons: the envy of the unbelievers, who did not want prophets sent to anyone other than their own peoples; the grudges and hatreds of the Jews; and the "deviance" and "sinfulness" of both communities, which made them unwilling to admit that Muhammad might be right, especially when he pointed out their corruption.[14] This intentional malice puts the guilt for the original confrontation between Muhammad and the Jews/Christians solely on the "people of the book." Later jihadis have stressed that the Jews and Christians were the military aggressors as well, thus making these communities the instigators of both the intellectual and physical sides of the "eternal" struggle.

A second way of viewing the conflict between Islam and the rest of the world is through the lens of the Qur'anic word taghut (tyranny).[15] By identifying leaders of the liberal West—men like Bush, Blair, or Berlusconi—with this religious term, the jihadis are able to claim that they share the characteristics of the tyrants mentioned in the sacred texts. They can then argue that, as with Pharaoh and other godless oppressors of the Qur'an and hadith, so the unbelievers today want to dominate the world. The tyrants know—as did Pharaoh—that the Truth, opposed to tyranny and oppression by its very nature and calling, is the only obstacle to these plans. Therefore, they know that they must get rid of Islam and the faithful Muslims if their wicked designs are to succeed. This syllogism again allows jihadis to seek answers for how to deal with the conflict by turning to the Qur'an and hadith.

The final concept was also first raised by Qutb and now finds wide acceptance among many jihadist groups. The basic idea is that various nations and peoples have embodied unbelief throughout time. The first representatives of unbelief were, of course, the Jews and early Christians. Once they were prevented from fulfilling their plans, the Christian West (initially represented by the Byzantine Empire), embarked on a vicious war against the Islamic community in an attempt to wipe it out. Only the superior strategies and military acumen of Muhammad and his successors prevented this from happening. When Byzantium faltered, Rome stepped in and began the Crusades as a holy war against Islam itself. The aim of the Crusades was thus not to prevent attacks on pilgrims, to support Constantinople in its war with various Islamic states, nor to táke back Jerusalem from the Saracens, but rather to destroy Islam and kill or convert all the Muslims. The failure of the Crusades to achieve this objective led directly to imperialism and the colonization of Islamic territory, viewed by the jihadis as simply another attempt by the unbelievers to destroy Islam. The five-hundred-year gap between the ending of the Crusades and the start of French and British incursions into Egypt is, by the way, glossed over as if it does not exist. To eliminate Islam, the Christian colonizers used every wicked tool at their disposal (missionary activity, Westernized education, the imposition of French and British legal systems) but were miraculously prevented from harming the true religion. With the collapse of the European empires, the

United States took up the cause and—through its ideology of liberalism—is now the leading spirit behind the attempts by falsehood to destroy Islam and kill or convert the Muslims. Modern jihadist groups recognize the new position of the United States by calling it the "greater Unbelief (Kufr)," an important term taken from the work of Ibn Taymiyya that will be explored in greater depth later. Jihadis stress that this latest chapter in the struggle between Truth and falsehood/unbelief may not be the last, because the conflict is destined to continue until the end of time, when final victory will come to the Muslims.

Each of these embodiments of unbelief has had its own strategies and tactics for attacking Muslims that the jihadis do not see as distinct assaults motivated by specific circumstances, but rather as part of the overall conspiracy to destroy Islam. This "campaign to suppress Islam," as one jihadist group calls it, began with military and smear attacks by the earliest Jews and Christians. Militarily, jihadis believe that the two communities attacked the early believers whenever they could and were traitorous when they signed treaties. The jihadis also see an ideological side to the campaign, claiming that Jews and Christians distorted the message of Muhammad, blasphemed against God, and denied the prophethood of the founder of Islam. These two sides to the earliest assault on Islam—one military and the other ideological—created a precedent for later attacks that the jihadis believe the enemies of Islam have followed ever since.

The Crusades, in contrast, were a strictly military attempt to conquer Islamic lands and kill or forcibly convert Muslims. According to Hizb al-Tahrir, European Christians had carefully watched the situation in the Caliphate and waited patiently to attack until the Islamic state was sufficiently weak. When various provinces of the state had managed to break off and begin independent lives, they realized that the time was ripe for conquest.[16] To achieve their nefarious ends, the Crusaders chose a specific strategy of creating in Islamic territory Christian states that would then gradually expand until they took over the entire Muslim community. Jihadis believe that only the dedication to Islam of the Muslims living at that time, and the brave leadership of Salah al-Din, saved the Islamic world from destruction.[17]

There are two implications that jihadis draw from the experience of the Crusades. First and foremost is the idea of the crusades as archetype. Just as certain figures and stories from the Qur'an and hadith repeat themselves throughout history, so too are the Crusades seen as teaching important permanent lessons about the unbelievers and how to defeat them. In its founding manifesto, Hamas states that the group takes very seriously the "lessons" to be learned from the Crusades, most especially that Muslims can face these "raids" and plan how to fight and defeat them "provided that the intentions are pure, the determination is true and that Muslims have benefited from past experiences, rid themselves of the effects of ideological invasion[18] and followed the customs of their ancestors."[19] Hizb al-Tahrir believes the Crusades teach Muslims that true victory will come only if the unbelievers are expelled from Islamic lands and the Muslims then follow up with further conquests and wars against the unbelievers in their own lands.[20] Other jihadis argue that the choice of strategies by the Crusaders, the creation of dependent states that would act as bridgeheads within the Islamic community, has reappeared with the setting up of the artificial Crusader state of Israel.[21] This is one reason that Qutb, 'Usama bin Ladin, and other jihadis call their current enemies "Zionist-Crusaders."

The second implication is that the Crusades never really ended.[22] Although pushed out of the Middle East by the Islamic fervor of faithful Muslims and by Salah al-Din, the Europeans were only rebuffed and not truly defeated. All the interactions of Europeans (and Americans) with the Islamic world after the Middle Ages are seen as continuations of the "crusading spirit," which is attempting to finish off the offensive begun hundreds of years before.[23] Qutb believed that "all Westerners" carried this spirit "in their blood," and that it was their hatred of Islam that motivated their attempts to conquer and colonize the Muslims in the nineteenth and twentieth centuries[24] through what he called "crusaderist imperialism."[25] Qutb linked the imperial impulse as well to "international Zionism," which fought together with the Christians in an unjust war against the only obstacle to their plans for world domination: Islam.[26] He warned that Muslims should not be confused by arguments that the Europeans were no longer motivated by religious feelings, because "when we talk about crusader hostility toward Islam latent in the European soul, we must not be deceived by appearances. We must not be fooled by the pretense of respect for religious freedom or the claim that Europe is not fanatically Christian today as it was at the time of the crusades, so that there is nothing to drive them to fanaticism against Islam as there was in those days. This is all deception and error."[27] Imperialism was not primarily about economic resources, control of territory, or military domination, but instead, like the Crusades, was about the destruction of Islam.[28] Even more telling was his attack on modern Western scholars who attempted to show that the Crusades were a form of imperialism. This was exactly backward, Qutb wrote: "The truth of the matter is that the latter-day imperialism is but a mask for the crusading spirit, since it is not possible for it to appear in its true form, as it was possible in the Middle Ages."[29]

Some jihadis, while not rejecting the identification of the Crusades with imperialism, have found other ways to understand this European/Christian/Jewish assault on Islam. A common interpretation, almost certainly influenced by exposure to leftist critiques, condemns the capitalist exploitation of Muslim countries: the purposeful oppression and humiliation visited on colonized territory to steal the wealth of the Muslims and to enrich the imperial center.[30] A word of caution is in order, however, since many jihadis—including Hizb al-Tahrir, al-Muhajiroun, and Supporters of Shari'ah—use the term capitalist to mean secular liberalism or even democracy. The charge then is not just that the Europeans exploited and oppressed Islamic lands for financial gain (as the general leftist analysis would have it), but that these "Jews and Christians" stole the wealth of the Muslims and imposed their ideas about modernity, democracy, and liberalism in a deliberate attempt to destroy Islam. The charge against the Jews is made explicitly by Hamas. In its manifesto the group asserts that "with their money they [the Jews] were able to control imperialistic countries and instigate them to colonize many countries in order to enable them to exploit their resources and spread corruption there."[31] The corruption, of course, includes the subversive ideas, such as liberalism, of the Western world.

Jihadis argue, in fact, that the political and economic aspects of imperialism were, right from the start, combined with an ideological assault on the religion, led by missionaries and orientalists. The imperialist powers set up universities to launch fierce campaigns against "Islamic thoughts" and to shift the allegiance of Muslim students to Western ways of thinking. Western culture was to replace Islamic culture, Western laws were to make obsolete Islamic laws, Muslims were to learn to criticize and even despise their own history and to favor Western history. Meanwhile, orientalists made Muslims doubt their religion by subjecting the Qur'an and hadith to critical analysis while missionaries attempted to convert them to Christianity.[32] As discussed earlier, Sayyid Qutb and Hasan al-Banna were especially sensitive to the ideological assault on Islam.[33] In his commentary on the Qur'an, Qutb denounced the leading intellectuals of his time, arguing that they had been brainwashed by orientalist critiques of their religion and then implanted by Westerners into the Islamic community in a deliberate attempt to ruin Islam.[34] The unbelievers did not study Islam as a way to understand and appreciate the religion, he wrote, but rather to find its weaknesses and attack it so that they could draw Muslims away from the true faith.[35]

Sayyid Qutb argued that the ideological conflict showed the real essence of the confrontation between the Muslim community and the "Judeo-Christian world." Despite the physical control of the colonizers, he would write, the confrontation was not over territory or for military domination, but rather it was a struggle whose sole aim was to destroy Islam.[36] Because the war was first and foremost one of faith and belief, it was obvious that the enemies of Islam would have to lead the believers astray from their religion and even to deceive them about the true nature of the conflict.[37] In the end, however, the orientalists and missionaries were unable to remove the "solid rock" of Islam, forcing Europeans to find another way to destroy the religion.[38]

On 3 March 1924 they finally succeeded, carrying out what one jihadi has called "the mother of all crimes": the abolition of the Caliphate.[39] In the jihadist understanding of this catastrophe, the imperialists wanted to dismantle the Caliphate primarily because their enmity for Islam compelled them to do so, and not for imperial profit. Kemal Atatürk was thus the tool of the Jews and British and French colonialists, who used him to strike a decisive blow against the only entity that could uphold the rules and laws of Islam.[40] The proof of this, jihadis argue, can be seen in the European demand that the shari'a be eliminated and replaced with European laws, and that a secular state be established in the place of the righteous Caliphate.[41] Atatürk, through this reading of history, becomes an "English agent," "Jewish criminal," and "traitor to Islam," wholly controlled and manipulated by the unbelievers for their evil schemes.[42] Many jihadis agree that since the day that the Caliphate was abolished, "Islam has disappeared from the living of life."[43]

With the destruction of the Caliphate, the imperialists could move on to implement the other elements of their anti-Islamic conspiracy. One of the most important of these was to divide up the Caliphate (which the jihadists claim included the entire Islamic world) into "cartoon states," "measly pieces" that they could more easily manipulate.[44] All these petty states—set up on "nationalist, democratic, capitalist or communist models of 'progress' and 'development,'" are not only un-Islamic, they are in fact actively opposed to Islam, serving the global purposes of unbelief.[45] To compound the problem, the imperialist powers put subservient agent rulers in charge of the ministates so that they could maintain their control of Islamic territory even after direct colonization had ended.[46] These deceiving leaders conspire with "their masters" the unbelievers to help the West dominate the world, follow Western directives in all their domestic and foreign policies, and, most importantly, oppress the real Muslims and keep "true" Islam from being implemented.[47] The heads of most of the Gulf states, the Hashamite rulers of Jordan, Pervez Musharraf, and Husni Mubarak are specifically named as agents of the British, Americans, and other Western powers.[48] The most hated of the "puppets," however, is the Saudi regime.[49] Hizb al-Tahrir even argues that not only the original Saudi leader, but his spiritual adviser, 'Abd al-Wahhab, were agents of the British in the unbelievers' struggle to undermine and eventually destroy the Ottoman Empire.[50]

Al-Qaida agrees with this reading of the leaders in Islamic countries. 'Usama bin Ladin has long attacked the Saudi ruling family for their abandonment of Islamic law, persecution of the "true" Muslims, economic policies that devastated his homeland, and support for the Americans.[51] As we shall see, it was the latter that would eventually inform his decision to declare war on the United States in 1996. Bin Ladin has also called the heads of Pakistan and "some Arab countries" American agents.[52] An al-Qaida statement from November 2002 accuses the United States of using their Islamic agent rulers to prevent the establishment of shari'a, to humiliate and imprison the real Muslims, to steal the Islamic community's wealth, and to surrender to the Jews. Meanwhile, when the Islamic party in Algeria practiced democracy and won the elections, "you unleashed your agents in the Algerian army on to them, to attack them with tanks and guns, to imprison them and torture them."[53]

The dismantling of the European empires and the collapse of overt imperialism has not, in the minds of the jihadis, ended this

Western strategy in the war against Islam. Russia, France, and Britain are still assumed to be colonial powers, intent on re-asserting their control over the Islamic lands and on resuming their assault on Islam.[54] In the same way, despite the fact that the United States was never involved in imperialist ventures in the Middle East or in any Islamic territory, Americans are also called colonizers who have the same goals as the Europeans. The jihadis believe that the only difference is that the United States has been more cunning in disguising its intentions, engaging in cultural imperialism rather than military or political domination. Using various slogans such as "humanitarian intervention," and the promise of military accords, mutual security agreements, economic and financial aid, and cultural programs, the United States is insinuating itself into the weak countries that make up the Islamic community in order to dominate and control them.[55]

Jihadis also believe that one true colonial state remains in the Middle East: Israel. As we have already seen, the founding of Israel is taken by jihadis as a continuation of the Crusader strategy of planting Western states on Islamic territory. Israel is thus seen as part of the military assault by the West to "subjugate a portion of the Muslim world permanently."[56] A further elaboration of this point argues that Israel has three distinct strategic purposes, all serving the interests of Britain and other colonizers: to separate "the Muslim lands in the East from those in the West, making their unity more difficult"; to plant "a new enemy for the

Muslims on their lands, in the first Qiblah [direction of prayer] and the third of the Holiest Mosques. This would draw their attention to a new enemy, focusing all their energies on defeating him and in turn weakening their capability of resisting Western aggression"; and to establish "an advanced base for the disbelieving colonialists" for their further conquests and schemes.[57] Ayman Zawahri and 'Usama bin Ladin tie this aggression—the founding and continued existence of Israel—to the United States specifically. Zawahri argued that "Israel is a developed American military base in the heart of the Islamic world and in one of its most sacred places. So America must pay the price for its oppressive and brutal policy toward the Muslims, especially in Palestine."[58] For bin Ladin, the United States and Israel are so intertwined that to talk about "Israel" or the Jews is to talk about America.[59] He in fact declared after the September 11 attacks that "those who distinguish between America and Israel are the real enemies of the [Islamic] nation."[60] It is interesting that Khomeini agreed with this reading of the relationship between Israel and the United States long before the Six-Days War.[61] The support of the United States explains for jihadis how small Israel has been able to defeat the combined might of the Islamic nation for the past fifty years.[62]

The existence of Israel has other sinister implications, connected to the supposedly ancient struggle with the Jews. At least one jihadist group argues that Israel is part of a Jewish attempt to recapture the lands and honor that were lost 1,400 years ago when Muhammad defeated Jewish Arab tribes in places like Khaybar.[63] Many more believe that "Zionists" want to expand their current territory until it includes most of the Middle East, creating a "Greater Israel" that—in conjunction with the United States—will eventually try to rule the world.[64] The entire campaign against Iraq (1991–present) is viewed as part of the overall Jewish/American plot to disarm any potential enemies of Israel and ensure Israeli dominance in the Middle East as the first step in this long-term strategy.[65] Other jihadis have accepted European anti-Semitic motifs and see Israel in control of media around the globe, behind every war, and, above all, continually attacking and corrupting Islam.[66]

Israel is supported in its drive to corrupt Islam by a fresh ideological assault on the religion from the West.[67] Dissatisfied with the results of the missionary and orientalist offensive, "unbelief" had to find other ways to destroy Islam and the Islamic way of life. The new attack has some of the elements of the old (such as questioning the truthfulness of Islam and attempting to distort the sacred texts), but it has several additional elements designed to undermine a Muslim "mentality,"[68] including a coordinated assault through the international media, an attack by scientists on the truth of the Qur'an and hadith, and the promotion of a series of Western concepts meant to confuse and demoralize Muslims. Using newspapers, TV, satellite dishes, radio, and the Internet, the unbelievers hope to destroy the morality that forms the bedrock of Islamic society.[69] After exposure to debauched

TV shows like *Baywatch*, Internet pornography, music, dance, and other temptations, Muslims abandon their religious duties—the prayer—and adopt the wicked and un-Islamic behavior of the United States and the rest of the West.[70] An American jihadi is not alone when he laments the media's "promotion of a degenerate counterculture" that has "corrupted our youth and robbed us of a whole generation of future leaders."[71] In one of his audiotapes, bin Ladin protests "the crusader media campaigns against the Islamic nation. These campaigns show how malicious are the evils they harbor against the nation in general and against the people of the two holy mosques in particular. The Americans' intentions have also become clear in statements about the need to change the beliefs, curricula, and morals of Muslims to become more tolerant, as they put it. In clearer terms, it is a religious-economic war. They want the believers to desist from worshipping God so that they can enslave them, occupy their countries, and loot their wealth."[72] Other "unbelieving" states participate in the West's attack on Islam, including India, indicted by Kashmiri jihadis for opening up theaters and otherwise spreading corrupt behavior.[73]

A second part of this coordinated offensive has been undertaken by Western scientists, who have apparently worked with political and religious leaders to find the perfect ways to threaten the totalizing truth of Islam. Western scientific ideas like evolution, psychology, and sociology, which create doubt in the minds of the Muslims about their faith, are purposely disseminated through Western-style education in the Islamic world. On this particular part of the ideological assault, one jihadi writes that "Muslims must remember that the Qur'an is the truth and if scientists contradict what the Qur'an says, then Allah . . . and the Qur'an [are] still correct and they are liars."[74]

The West has promulgated too a number of devious concepts—"interfaith dialogue," "integration," "tolerance," and "multiculturalism"—specifically designed to reduce a Muslim's attachment to the community and Islamic ideals, while convincing Muslims that other religions and cultures are the equal of Islam.[75] The West used "nationalism," on the other hand, to split up the community on racial or ethnic grounds and thus weaken the entire Islamic world.[76] Likewise, jihadis insist that the notions of "moderate Muslims" and "fundamentalist Muslims" are a Western invention meant to create divisions within the umma and thus destroy its greatest strength: the unity of all Muslims.[77] Fundamentalism is a particular bugbear for the jihadis, who recognize that this label has cost them prestige in the eyes of moderate Muslims.[78] Three general lines of argument are to assert that all true Muslims—including Muhammad—are, by the West's definition, fundamentalists; that without the fundamentalists Islam would have been destroyed long ago; and that in any case this is an artificial category created by the West to attack the true Muslims.[79] The related campaign against terrorists and terrorism has led to two separate responses. Some jihadis embrace the terms, arguing that the Qur'an and hadith command the believers to terrorize their enemies while others see this as just another slur used to malign the only tactics that Muslims have to wage war on the unbelieving oppressors.[80] 'Usama bin Ladin's views on this particular concept have changed over time. In 1996 and 1998 he argued that the United States used the label "terrorist" to divert attention from the true state terrorism that it regularly practiced on Muslims in Iraq and elsewhere,[81] while after September 11 he asserted that there was "good terrorism" and "bad terrorism," and that "we practice terrorism that is a good feat, which deters [the United States and Israel] from killing our children in Palestine and other places."[82]

The assault on Islamic thoughts is complemented by American manipulation of Muslims' education. In recent years, the U.S. government has quietly requested that certain intolerant aspects of schoolbooks in places like the Palestinian Authority and Saudi Arabia be altered. These requests are attacked by jihadis (and many Islamists and Wahhabis) as unwarranted interference in the internal affairs of the Islamic nation.[83] For jihadis there is only one reason for the American efforts at educational reform: to seize control of young Muslims and shape their minds as the unbelievers wish.[84] A jihadist professor argues that this insidious plot "is a crime against the coming generations, destroying their mentalities and spirit, and in the end, it will lead to the complete overpowering of their Islamic personalities, producing generations of Muslims molded by the West, attached to her [religion], [creed], values and system of life."[85] In a revealing declaration

that shows just how seriously some jihadis take educational reform, al-Qaida demanded, in a statement from November 2002,
"Do not interfere in our politics and method of education. Leave
us alone, or else expect us in New York and Washington."[86]

Jihadis believe that the United States and the rest of the
West are not alone in their ideological offensive against Islam.
Government-appointed ulama and other Islamic scholars, for
financial or political gain, have perverted their calling and loyalty to Islam by issuing fatwas in support of un-Islamic behavior.[87] Respected shaikhs like Wahhabi 'Abd al-'Aziz Bin Baz
and Islamist Yusuf al-Qaradhawi are bitterly attacked as "mis-
tresses to the satanic rulers" and "Pentagon Muslims," willing to
undermine the rule of God's law to keep their favored standing
within the governments of the "puppet agents."[88] Denigrating
even Islamist scholars who disagree with their vision of Islam, jihadis have cut themselves loose from any authority that might be
able to limit their war and will trust only their own particular interpretations of the texts.

According to jihadis, after decades of ideological attacks the
West believed that they had prepared the grounds for a final all-
out military offensive on Islam. Using their surrogates, the Israelis and Maronites, the United States was already killing Palestinian and Lebanese Muslims. Then the Americans for the first
time inserted their own troops into the fight, invading Beirut
with the colonialist French to put down the Islamic rising against
the Christians and Jews. Although chased away (surprisingly eas-

ily) by the actions of a few brave Muslims, the Americans did not give up. The United States (with the UN) attacked Saddam Hussain in 1991—and used the resulting sanctions to kill millions of Muslim children; they invaded Somalia and tried to take over the country; Americans armed and incited Serbs in Bosnia and Kosovo; and the United States and other unbelievers aided multiple attacks on Muslims around the world—in Kashmir, Chechnya, Indonesia, Sudan, and elsewhere.[89] For 'Usama bin Ladin and other jihadis, the final blow was the Saudi welcoming of American troops into the holiest territory of Islam and the "land of the two sacred mosques."[90] In his 1996 declaration of war and 1998 reiteration, bin Ladin made the presence of American soldiers in the Arabian peninsula his main casus belli, claiming that this was a de facto occupation of Islamic land and therefore completely unacceptable to Islamic law.[91]

The breadth of the campaign against Islam is staggering, involving every single nation on the planet as well as every international organization.[92] Qutb called the unbelieving forces "a grand alliance of evil," unified only by their hatred for Muslims and their desire to see the believers dead and Islam destroyed.[93] At the head of the offensive, always leading the way in the attacks on Muslims and Islam worldwide, is the United States. By the nineties America became for jihadis the source of every evil, the fountainhead of the unbelief that has always tried to destroy Islam.[94] Yet all was not lost. The jihadis argued that "as the democrats seek to extend their reach, the Muslim world has, at last, begun its defense, paving the way for the inevitable war between Islam and Kufr."[95] The jihad has begun and it can end only with the destruction of the evil powers, the overthrow of their wicked ideology of liberalism, and the downfall of their unlawful international system.

6 *The Clash of Civilizations, Part II*

To jihadis, the aggression of the unbelievers, their ideological assault, and the military conflicts that they have begun, justify open warfare with them. The term that the extremists use for this warfare, *jihad*, has been discussed earlier, but there are details about the concept that need further clarification. As we have seen, the majority of the *ahadith* (plural of hadith) and verses in the Qur'an that deal with the topic refer to jihad as fighting (*qital*). There is also a well-developed body of work within Islamic jurisprudence (fiqh) that treats jihad as fighting and elaborates a legal framework for this Islamic just war. Each of the four schools of fiqh (Maliki, Hanifi, Hanbali and Shafi'i) has rules and regulations for participating in jihad: when it is legitimate and when not; who is bound to participate and who can be excused; what behaviors and tactics are acceptable. A brief look at "The

Reliance of the Traveler," one of the older Shafi'i manuals of shari'a (written in 1368) shows this traditional view of jihad: that it is primarily about fighting; that the fighting will continue until everyone in the world acknowledges the rule of Islam; that fighting is a communal obligation (*fard kifayya*) when offensive and an individual obligation (fard 'ayn) when defensive.[1] Jihad can be declared only by the Caliph in this traditional vision of Islamic just war, a requirement that has created difficulty for jihadis today. The objective of jihad in the manual is to make war on the Jews, Christians, and Zoroastrians until they acknowledge the rule of Islam and pay tribute, or until they become Muslims. Other peoples (including polytheists and apostates from Islam) have only the choice of becoming Muslim or dying. The extremists are therefore not outside the bounds of *traditional* Islam when they talk about jihad as warfare justified by certain criteria.

Yet the way that the radicals talk about jihad does not fit within *modern* Islamic discourse about this sensitive duty. The general Islamic understanding of jihad today is that it consists of both an internal and an external component. Believers are urged to strive for a deeper faith and to control their desires, while seeking God and the good. This internal struggle is given priority, but there is also a vision of external struggle that includes striving to make society conform to Islamic norms of justice. The warfare that forms the majority of the verses and ahadith on the subject of jihad is understood by present-day Muslims to refer to a specific time and place during Muhammad's mission, a time that has come and gone. Instead Muslims believe that the just war of jihad is defensive only, the last resort when attacked by aggressors.[2] Jihadis have subverted this modern understanding of jihad and are attempting to win over the Muslim community to their vision of continuous warfare with the unbelievers by making jihad as fighting the only definition of jihad; by defining their jihad as defensive or at least as legitimated by respected Islamic scholars; and by justifying the way they fight their war with legal rulings from religious authorities past and present.

Perhaps most importantly, jihadis ignore or minimize the internal struggle that is part of the concept of jihad. The Qur'an uses the phrase "jihad fi sabil Allah" (struggle in the cause of God) in ways that have nothing to do with fighting, and the text often employs the term *jihad* in the sense of working to do God's will.[3] Even when striving with the unbelievers is mentioned, there are verses that describe this as a struggle with words only, not with weapons.[4] The term *mujahidun* is also used at times to refer to those who strive in good deeds, and not to warriors.[5] The most important hadith on the internal jihad quotes Muhammad as saying after a significant victory by the Muslims that "we have returned from the lesser jihad to the greater jihad." When asked by his companions what was the "greater jihad," Muhammad is reported to have replied, "The struggle within one's own soul." Most Muslims accept this hadith as valid and see it as legitimating a turn away from the earlier emphasis on warfare and toward the internal struggle for goodness. The jihadis, along with some

Islamists, reject this hadith as spurious and have spilled a great deal of ink trying to show why warfare cannot be the "lesser jihad."[6] Throughout their writings jihad as fighting (qital) dominates and for many becomes the whole of this duty.[7] Then, in turn, warfare becomes the whole of Islam. For jihadis, combat on the path of God is the same as their faith and the entirety of their religion. The other duties (prayer, tithing, fasting, the hajj) may even take second place to warfare, which is the "peak" of the religion and compulsory on true Muslims.[8] They agree with Ibn Taymiyya that those Muslims who refuse to take part in the fighting are at the very least hypocrites who have neglected the faith and perhaps even apostates who can be fought and killed.[9]

The issue of defensive warfare is more complicated. As we have seen, jihadis argue that the struggle facing Muslims began with attacks by the West, an argument that is designed to convince doubting Muslims that they should join the battle against open aggression, the only good reason for war that most of the Islamic community now recognizes. That the vast majority of Muslims have not taken up arms suggests that the extremists have failed to win their argument. There is another tack taken by certain jihadist groups: to define "defensive" in creative ways that allow them a great deal of latitude in making their case.[10] Both Mawdudi and Qutb argued that the difference between offensive and defensive did not make sense in Islamic jihad—only the difference between an individual and a collective duty. Faced with criticism from liberal Muslims, however, both had to find a way to deal with these categories. Mawdudi tried to convince Indian Muslims that a distinction between the terms *offensive* and *defensive* could be made only when one nation attacked another in pursuit of territorial gain. Islam, in contrast, sought to assault the rule of an opposing ideology (an offensive attack) while defending its own principles through capturing state power (an offensive tactic but with a defensive purpose).[11] Sayyid Qutb, confronted by Islamic clergy who insisted that Islam recognized only defensive warfare as just, wrote, "If we insist on calling Islamic Jihad a defensive movement, then we must change the meaning of the word 'defense' and mean by it 'the defense of man' against all those elements which limit his freedom. These elements take the form of beliefs and concepts, as well as of political systems, based on economic, racial or class distinctions. . . . When we take this broad meaning of the word 'defense,' we understand the true character of Islam, and that it is a universal proclamation of the freedom of man from servitude to other men, the establishment of the sovereignty of God and His Lordship throughout the world, the end of man's arrogance and selfishness, and the implementation of the rule of the Divine Shari'ah in human affairs."[12] Defensive jihad for Qutb then becomes a war for the freedom of man from servility to other men, a war that allows people to become the slaves of God alone.

The definition of "defensive" by Qutb and Mawdudi shows that they envisioned aggression as the mere existence of competing ideologies, rather than a physical attack by an enemy state or other entity. Later jihadist theorists, such as Fathi Yakan, had similarly unusual definitions for aggression. In a section of his book devoted to "self-defense," Yakan discussed the necessity of jihad to counter "attacks from every materialistic ideology and system that threatens the existence of Islam as a global paradigm of thought and system of life."[13] In their explication of the "clash of civilizations," Hizb al-Tahrir begins with the "violent intellectual struggle" unleashed by the West and then discusses the economic and political aggression that continued throughout the twentieth century.[14] There are several specific cases of nonviolent interaction with unbelievers that the jihadis have argued are, in fact, aggression. Thus bin Ladin believed that the U.S. humanitarian intervention in Somalia during 1992–1993 "was a blatant invasion under the eyes of the whole world. Somalia was occupied for crusader-colonialist purposes," and therefore grounds for jihad.[15] Yet another unusual definition of aggression is the persecution of Muslims by the unbelievers, also called "oppression" in the Qur'an.[16] Hindering anyone from accepting Islam, intimidating Muslims, or treating the believers unjustly is viewed by jihadis as reason enough for defensive jihad.[17]

A more widely accepted view of aggression is when Islamic lands are physically invaded, conquered, or occupied. Almost every Islamic scholar advocates defensive jihad in these circumstances, and most Islamists also see this as the proper definition for aggression and justification therefore for declaring a jihad.[18] The four schools of fiqh describe an attack by the unbelievers as one of the major reasons for jihad to become an individual duty (fard 'ayn), meaning that every male Muslim is obligated by his religion to join the defensive struggle against the invaders. Even Hizb al-Tahrir, which has supposedly renounced jihad until the creation of an Islamic state, believes in joining a jihad if an Islamic country is invaded.[19] When bin Ladin declared war on the United States in 1996 based on the fact that the Americans had invaded Muslim countries (Iraq and Arabia) and were occupying the holy lands of the Hijaz, he was tapping into this general Islamic understanding of aggression in hopes of rallying Muslims to his cause.[20]

Yet there are several complicating factors even in this concept. Before 1492, distinguishing Islamic lands from those of the unbelievers was fairly straightforward. Various Muslim rulers controlled parts of Spain, North Africa, the Middle East, and beyond to India and Indonesia. This entire area was, by definition, the Islamic lands. Matters have become more complex since. The question is what, in the modern world, constitutes "Islamic territory." Most Muslims today believe that this means the same thing as Islamic nations, and consists of those countries where Muslims are a clear majority. The jihadis vehemently disagree. 'Umar Bakri Mohammad, the leader of al-Muhajiroun, defines Islamic territory as "any place Islam conquered or where Islam was implemented or where the majority of people embraced Islam on it. If the signs of Islam become prevalent e.g. [the call to worship] and [Ramadan] celebrations, then it will become a

Muslim country."[21] By this definition, a country does not have to be mostly Muslim to become an Islamic country—it need only have a large number of Muslims residing within its boundaries or have been under an Islamic state at any point in history. Keeping this territory from unbelieving domination then becomes an obligation, and defensive jihad is justified. This explains why Palestine as a whole is considered invaded, conquered, and occupied territory by the jihadis.[22] In the same vein, the jihadis in Kashmir engage in warfare because, they argue, India invaded and occupied Islamic territory when the ruler of Kashmir declared his intention to turn his state over to India and not Pakistan.[23]

Hasan al-Banna was the one of the first proponents of this view. He recognized a "minor homeland" consisting of Egypt and the Sudan, a "great homeland" of the Arab-speaking Muslim world, and a "greater homeland" of the Muslim world from the Atlantic Ocean to the Indian Ocean, all of which had to be liberated from the occupying infidels.[24] In his basic work on the obligation for Muslims to wage jihad in Afghanistan to repel the Soviet invaders, 'Azzam was just as adamant about the need to reconquer every bit of Islamic land that had been taken from the Islamic community. He wrote that "if the [unbelievers] infringe upon a hand span of Muslim land, jihad becomes [an individual duty] for its people and for those near by. . . . Sin is suspended to the necks of all Muslims as long as any hand span of land that was Islamic is in the hands of the [unbelievers]." But what land was he talking about? He explained that "the sin upon this present generation, for not advancing towards Afghanistan, Palestine, the Philippines, Kashmir, Lebanon, Chad, Eritrea etc[.], is greater than the sin inherited from the loss of the lands which have previously fallen into the possession of the [unbelievers]." By the previously occupied lands, 'Azzam meant that Spain, Bulgaria, and more must also at some point be reconquered through a defensive jihad.[25]

The inclusion of lands that have not been ruled by an Islamic state for generations in 'Azzam's definition of Islamic territory is not unusual. In an open letter to George W. Bush after September 11, Shaikh Safar al-Hawali, one of al-Qaida's supporters in Saudi Arabia, wrote that he and people like him still dreamed of "regaining" al-Andalus (Spain).[26] The jihadis who carried out the Madrid bombings of 11 March 2004 gave as one of their reasons the "Spanish crusade against the Muslims," (the *reconquista*) and that "it has not been so long since the expulsion from Al-Andalus and the courts of the Inquisition."[27] Hizb al-Tahrir claims the entire Balkans, Hungary, Romania, Austria, the Crimea, and Poland as eternal Islamic land for which a defensive jihad can be waged.[28] In a long treatise on jihad, the head of Jama'at ud-Dawa in Pakistan argued that "Spain that had been Muslim territory for more than eight hundred years was captured by the Christians. . . . Now it is our duty to restore Muslim rule to this land of ours. The whole of India, including Kashmir, Hyderabad, Assam, Nepal, Burma, Behar, and Junagadh was once a Muslim territory. But we lost this vast territory and it fell into the hands of the disbelievers just because we disregarded Jihad."[29] Other jihadis also support "retaking" all of India as well as Russia (which once paid tribute to the Muslim Tatars).[30]

The question of offensive jihad is even more complex and controversial. The most widely respected Islamic authorities: the six accepted collections of (Sunni) hadith; the authoritative commentators on, and exegetes of, the hadith and Qur'an; the leading ancient experts on Islamic law; and the four schools of Islamic fiqh all assume that Muslims have a duty to spread the dominion of Islam, through military offensives, until it rules the world. By the dominion of Islam these authorities did not mean that everyone in the world must convert to Islam, since they also affirmed that "there is no compulsion in religion," rather that every part of the earth must come under Islamic governance and especially the rule of the shari'a. 'Azzam's definition of offensive jihad follows this traditional understanding of jihad, noting that it is a duty for the leader of the Muslims "to assemble and send out an army unit into the land of war once or twice every year. Moreover, it is the responsibility of the Muslim population to assist him, and if he does not send an army he is in sin. And the Ulama have mentioned that this type of jihad is for maintaining the payment of [tribute]. The scholars of the principles of religion have also said: 'Jihad is [the call to Islam] with a force, and is obligatory to perform with all available capabilities, until there remains only Muslims or people who submit to Islam.'"[31] Once again it must be emphasized that 'Azzam's explanation of offensive jihad is simply a recounting of the interpretations of the most respected *traditional* Islamic authorities. To deny this fact would be to deny one of the main reasons that jihadis have gotten a hearing in so much of the Islamic world today.

However, the vast majority of Muslims today have renounced this concept of a continuous offensive against the unbelievers. They believe that Islam will spread peacefully and without conflict and that military jihad today is reserved for defensive purposes alone.[32] Jihadis bitterly assail this attitude as a sign that Muslims have surrendered to the ideas and ideals of the unbelievers, that they have, as Qutb put it "defeatist and apologetic mentalities."[33] He wrote elsewhere that those Muslims who try to defend Islam by arguing that (offensive) jihad is a matter of history and no longer valid or necessary "have undermined the very meaning and significance of jihad for the culture and history of Islam."[34] Other jihadis have been equally harsh. Khubiab Sahib, in a widely disseminated tract on the "essential provision of the mujahid," writes that a new generation of Muslim intellectuals are presenting a distorted picture of Islam when they portray the shining past of Islam—the conquest of India through jihad—in an apologetic and guilt-ridden manner.[35]

A number of the extremists believe that the definitions of jihad as defensive war alone, as well as the attempts to control how the sacred texts that speak to jihad are interpreted, are part of the unbelievers' plots against Islam. The West, in this view, understands the significance of jihad and thus conspires to distort its meaning and keep the believers from the Qur'an and other sacred texts because otherwise they might take up the just war against their enemies.[36] The jihadis emphasize continually that only through a comprehensive vision of jihad—offensive as well as defensive—will the Islamic world be able to protect Muslims who are under attack, throw off the dominion of the unbelievers and apostate Muslims, regain the lost honor and dignity of former years, and advance Islam until it rules the world.[37] This constant need to support their interpretations of offensive jihad shows that the extremists have not yet won their argument with moderate Muslims who are resisting the idea of warfare with the rest of the world.

Jihadis, however, unlike most Muslims, embrace offensive jihad and fiercely defend their "right" to spread the rule of Islam even if they are not attacked by the unbelievers first. There are four basic justifications that jihadis give for offensive jihad: to obey God's command; to make the word of God supreme; to open the nations for Islam; and to make certain that the Islamic community assumes its rightful position as leader of the world. Jihadis argue that the most important reason for Muslims to wage offensive jihad is because God has commanded it. Regardless of any other justifications for this act, fulfilling one's duty to God—a duty just like prayer, tithing, or fasting—should be the prime motivating factor for the true believer.[38] In fact, as we have seen, many jihadis argue that anyone who will not engage in offensive warfare in the cause of God has abandoned the faith.

The other justifications are taken just as seriously. The phrase "to make God's word[39] supreme" means that the true believers will fight to ensure that the creed, "There is no divinity but God," with its implications about tawhid and God's sole right to rule, is implemented. Qutb and Mawdudi are the two ideologues most associated with this concept, and they have influenced profoundly the jihadis who have followed them.[40] As we have already seen, Qutb did not believe that there was any use talking about the defensive side of jihad: the most important part of the just war was to defeat the reigning political, social, cultural, and religious systems of the world and replace them with the dominion of God alone. Jihadis today have also emphasized this reason for offensive warfare against the unbelievers. 'Usama bin Ladin gave several reasons for his 1996 declaration of war on the United States, including making God's word the highest and the infidel's word inferior.[41] Later statements by bin Ladin confirmed that he saw this as the essential reason for instigating war against the Jews and Christians especially.[42]

The phrase "opening the nations for Islam" is a traditional way of talking about jihad that has specifically Islamic connotations.[43] In the first instance, it means making certain that every country will allow the call to Islam to be made freely and without hindrance. In the *traditional* interpretation of this phrase, any nation that blocked the spread of Islam by interfering with Muslim missionaries or that would not allow its peoples to be exposed to the Islamic message were legitimate targets for attack.[44] Jihadist groups agree with this traditional view, one even defining the entire concept of jihad as "the removal of obstacles, by force if necessary, that stand between people and Islam."[45] The other definition for "opening the nations" is part of jihadist discourse alone, and shows the influence that modern movements like socialism and communism have had on the jihadis. In this reading, Islam is a liberation theology, determined to free men from oppression by other men and return God to His rightful place as the sole legislator. This could be done only with an offensive that would take on the leading powers of the day and, through military and ideological struggle, overthrow them. For al-Banna, the Muslims thus become an "army of salvation which would rescue humanity," and lead them to the path of truth.[46] Freeing Egypt from secularism and modernity was just the beginning, for al-Banna stated that "we will not stop at this point, but will pursue this evil force to its own lands, invade its Western heartland, and struggle to overcome it until all the world shouts by the name of the Prophet and the teachings of Islam spread throughout the world. Only then will Muslims achieve their fundamental goal, and there will be no more 'persecution'[47] and all religion will be exclusively for Allah."[48] Mawdudi, obviously influenced by the rhetoric of his day, called Islam "a revolutionary ideology and program which seeks to alter the social order of the whole world and rebuild it in conformity with its own tenets and ideals." The method used to carry out this revolutionary program was jihad through word if possible or through the sword when necessary.[49]

Qutb saw Islam as "a general declaration for the liberation of mankind," and that it must employ an "army of truth" to bring this philosophical declaration into practical existence.[50] Thus it was "immaterial whether the homeland of Islam . . . is in a condition of peace or whether it is threatened by its neighbors. When Islam strives for peace, its objective is not that superficial peace which requires that only that part of the earth where the followers of Islam are residing remain secure. The peace which Islam desires is that the religion (i.e. the law of the society) be purified for God, that the obedience of all people be for God alone, and that some people should not be lords over others."[51] How could Islam, he demanded, abandon the rest of mankind, leaving them to suffer servitude to lords other than God Almighty? Muslims therefore had to seize the initiative and attack the tyrannical systems physically to save humanity and free people throughout the world from servitude.[52]

The three main jihadist ideologues make clear a central point of the ongoing war with falsehood: that it will continue until Islam has "liberated" the entire world from darkness, tyranny, and servitude to mere men. Jihadis thus neither recognize national boundaries within the Islamic lands nor do they believe that the coming Islamic state, when it is created, should have permanent borders with the unbelievers.[53] The recognition of such boundaries would end the expansion of Islam and stop offensive jihad, both of which are transgressions against the laws of God that command jihad to last until Judgment Day or until the entire earth is under the rule of Islamic law.[54] It would also prevent the Islamic nation from becoming the "best community brought forth for mankind," a Qur'anic injunction that they interpret as meaning that Muslims have been given the leadership of the entire planet.[55]

At the core of the extremists' views of jihad is their conviction that this is an act of worship dedicated to God alone. Thus jihadis believe that they must conduct both the offensive and defensive war according to the laws of Islam as found in the sacred texts, their earliest interpretations, and Islamic jurisprudence. The tactics that the jihadis use are chosen therefore because the extremists believe that these authorities permit or even prescribe them. It bears repeating that most Muslims disagree with the jihadist interpretation of the sacred texts and Islamic law, and especially their views on how to conduct offensive combat. The extremists do not, of course, care what the rest of the Islamic world has to say about jihad. They believe that they are maintaining the truth even if "so-called" Muslims have long since fallen into apostasy and sin.

Given the extremists' peculiar views of the sacred texts, jihadist warfare has taken on distinctive characteristics, including a belief in retaliation in kind, an idea that the essence of warfare is deception, and the use of suicide (martyrdom) operations. The Qur'an and the hadith support the notion of justice in retaliation, exemplified by the *lex talionis* (law of retaliation) and there is explicit support for attacking someone in the same way that he attacks the believers.[56] Jihadis have taken this to mean that just as the Americans and the rest of the West have aggressed against the Islamic world, the Muslim community has the God-given right to retaliate in kind: whatever weapons the enemy uses, the Muslims can use; whatever number of people the enemy kills, the Muslims have the right to kill an equivalent number. In the 1998 declaration of war, al-Qaida specifically called for killing civilians and military personnel based on the Qur'anic injunction to "fight the pagans all together as they fight you all together."[57] Two well-known jihadist clerics argued separately after the September 11 attack that the deaths of innocent civilians in New York was permitted because the United States had killed innocent Muslims.[58] The text cited by one of the clerics to justify this decision, "Then whoever transgresses the prohibition against you, you transgress likewise against him . . . may not necessitate the equality in the number of the dead or the wealth for this is a matter that cannot be specified in every case. But what is intended is to meet an action with an action: killing with killing, taking prisoners with taking prisoners and causing wreckage and destruction with causing wreckage and destruction."[59] Statements by bin Ladin, 'Ayman al-Zawahri, and other members of al-Qaida subsequently have all emphasized a supposed right to respond to any aggression in an equal manner.[60] Bin Ladin specifically said that "we treat others like they treat us. Those who kill our women and our innocent, we kill their women and innocent, until they stop from doing so," and that this was valid both religiously (because allowed by God and the shari'a) and logically (because retaliation would deter them from aggressing again).[61] Zawahri argued that Americans can also be treated the same as Israelis have treated the Palestinians, because the unbelievers were acting in concert with one another.[62]

A second jihadist tactic of war—deception—involves secrecy, speaking ambiguously, misleading the unbelievers, or even outright lying. This can include concealing one's allegiance to Islam and attacking the enemy without warning or declaring war (as long as they have at some time been invited to Islam).[63] The jihadis defend this sort of behavior with a well-known hadith by Muhammad that "war is deceit."[64] Since the extremists consider themselves always at war with the unbelievers and their Muslim agents, they also believe that they should always be allowed to lie to anyone who opposes their version of Islam. Some Westerners were surprised by the behavior of the September 11 hijackers just before they carried out their attacks, but their actions—pretending to be irreligious, acting as Americans would, and seemingly enjoying those sinful pleasures that the unbelievers do—could be justified by this principle of war.

The final tactic is much better known and includes the use of suicide bombers and the deaths of the hijackers during the September 11 attacks. The basic justification for this comes from a very traditional vision of Islamic law, which allows a warrior to carry out a hopeless assault if it will encourage the Muslims or cause the unbelievers to lose heart.[65] Respected clerics—

including non-jihadis—have endorsed suicide bombers as an effective and legitimate tactic, especially when used against Israelis, but also against Americans, Russians, and other non-Muslims.[66] Among the jihadist groups, Abu Hamza, Hizb al-Tahrir, and Zawahri have all explicitly approved these sorts of operations.[67] The jihadis believe that suicide bombers are effective because they strike fear into the hearts of the unbelievers, they show that the mujahidun love death rather than life, and they kill far more of the enemy than they do of the believers. They write off the "incidental" slaughter of innocents (including other Muslims) as unavoidable "collateral damage," which is, in any case, permitted by Islamic law.

It is this point that has created the most serious problems for the jihadis, for while the four traditional schools of shari'a have strict rules about what constitutes justified actions during war, these do not always match modern notions of legitimate military behavior. This was not always the case. Centuries before Western nations codified the international laws of war, Islamic jurisprudents used the Qur'an, hadith, and life of Muhammad to determine the Islamically correct way to conduct war. The majority determined that noncombatant women, children, and monks or nuns could not be killed; that captives should not be slaughtered outright; and that even animals and trees had certain rights.[68] Islamic law a thousand years ago was, in effect, beginning a process of distinguishing between military targets and civilians, protecting the rights of prisoners of war, and thinking about shielding the environment from the effects of war. The fact that Muslim nations became signatories to the various international conventions on warfare during the twentieth century and that the vast majority of Muslims today accept modern norms of behavior in wartime could be viewed as a natural continuation of this process.

The jihadis disagree. They have repeatedly stated that the very concept of international laws is contrary to the shari'a and refuse to honor any agreements between nations—including those that deal with military affairs, human rights, or international institutions and mechanisms. Instead they argue that Muslims need to return not only to the sacred texts, but also to the traditional interpretations of these texts to determine how to behave during military jihad today. The result has been actions that are recognized by the rest of the world—including the vast majority of Muslims—as outside the bounds of modern conventions of war. Five areas in particular are of special significance for understanding jihadist attacks over the past few decades: the targeting of civilians; the treatment of captives; an opposition to permanent peace treaties; the issue of booty; and terrorizing the enemy. The issue that clashes most strongly with the global view is the treatment of noncombatants. International law has very strict rules and definitions about how to distinguish civilians from soldiers and what constitutes legitimate military targets during time of war. The traditional Islamic understanding of belligerents did not follow these modern distinctions. Instead all four schools of fiqh agreed that all male unbelievers beyond puberty (generally age thirteen or fourteen) could be killed during jihad, regardless of whether they belonged to a formal military organization—even regardless of whether they had weapons. This does not mean that all males *had* to be killed: rather that, as a group, they were legitimate targets in time of war. The only exceptions to this rule were monks, old men (only in some of the schools of fiqh), the insane, and the disabled. Men from these groups, as well as women, children, and slaves were considered nonbelligerents who would not normally be killed unless they took up arms themselves, contributed money for the war, or incited fighting against the Muslims. Intentionally killing unbelievers who fell into one of the prohibited categories was not a serious sin, but rather an action that could be expiated by confession and prayer. Incidentally killing them—as well as Muslims—by using a weapon that killed indiscriminately, or because they were mixed in with combatants, was not even blameworthy.[69]

The jihadis affirm these medieval rules of warfare and therefore have no hesitation about killing any non-Muslim men who belong to the target country whether they are members of the military or not. Their definition of combatants is broad enough to allow as well the deliberate killing of women, children and Muslims if they help the enemy either by word or deed. Jihadis also justify killing these groups even if they are not helping the unbelievers when they are mixed with fighters, as long as they are not purposefully targeted.[70] The ideologue for the group that killed Egyptian president Anwar Sadat went one stop further and argued that deliberately killing Muslims was legal because the leading scholars of Islam allowed the killing of Muslim prisoners if the infidels used them as human shields or forced them to enlist in their army. If they are killed, he wrote, they will be martyrs, and the prescribed jihad cannot be neglected on account of those who are killed as martyrs. Hence, "when we kill them in accordance with the Command of God we are both rewarded and excused. They, however, will be judged according to their intentions."[71] As the September 11, Bali, and Madrid attacks show, al-Qaida and its clerical supporters have not been backward about endorsing military operations that either deliberately or incidentally kill noncombatants—including Muslims—based on these interpretations of the sacred texts.[72] Even before these occurred, bin Ladin supported attacks that led to the deaths of innocent Muslims and non-Muslims alike.[73] Other, non-Islamic, reasons are also given by some extremists for the killing of civilians. A Pakistani jihadi justified intentionally targeting all Indians because their population growth is a strategic threat to the Muslim community, while the Islamist Qaradhawi argued that Israeli civilians are legitimate military objectives because of both universal conscription and the democratic process that proves every Israeli is complicit in the policies of the government.[74] This same justification was given by one of al-Qaida's supporters for the killing of ordinary Americans during the September 11 attacks.[75]

The treatment of prisoners of war is a second area where jihadist views of legitimate warfare clash with current international norms. Governed by The Hague, Geneva, and other conventions, international law today recognizes that every combatant has the right to surrender and to receive good treatment from his captors, including the right to food, shelter, communication with the outside world, and freedom from torture. The traditional Islamic view was that the leader of the Muslims (the Caliph) had the right to choose four courses of action for male prisoners: death by "cutting the neck,"—slitting the throat or chopping off the head; enslavement; ransoming them for money, goods, or the release of Muslim prisoners; or freeing them. Female prisoners could only be enslaved or freed.[76] The jihadis again agree with these traditional views—although they have dismissed the need for a Caliph—and have been implementing them in their various conflicts.[77] The fact that Daniel Pearl, Nicholas Berg, Paul Johnson, and others were executed by having their throats cut was not a sign of lawlessness, but rather an indication of the jihadis' allegiance to these legal opinions. Again, when Masood Azhar bragged to a reporter about his success in obtaining weapons for the release of Indian captives, he was following his interpretation of the traditional judgments that allow ransoming prisoners of war for goods.[78] The issue of torture is addressed directly by al-Qaida, which argues from various ahadith that the scholars of Islam allow torture and beating hostages or other captives if it will help the Muslims.[79]

Jihadis also profess to follow the traditional Islamic rulings on peace treaties. The dominant model for jurisprudents' understanding of agreements with non-Muslims was Muhammad's treaty of Hudaybiyya. Here the Muslims and their opponents agreed to a cessation of hostilities that was to last ten years. Based on this precedent, Hanifi law recognized truces for up to ten years if "victory over [the unbelievers] and taking payment [of tribute] from them is too difficult to obtain." Jihad would resume without warning, however, if the non-Muslims broke the agreement.[80] Maliki law allowed truces for three months and then only if it is concluded for reasons other than fear alone.[81] The jihadis generally believe that cease-fires are possible under certain very circumscribed conditions, most especially that they do not allow unbelievers to have possession of Islamic land and that they have a definite time limit.[82] Qutb wrote that a truce could be declared without a specific period, but that "if treachery is *feared* on the part" of the unbelievers, it could be brought to an end.[83] Other jihadis and their clerical supporters are harsher. 'Umar Bakri Mohammad argues that in the absence of a "true" Islamic state, Muslims are not allowed to conclude any treaties with the unbelievers, while Hamas states in its covenant that no peaceful solution is possible with Israel.[84] There is also agreement that permanent peace with unbelievers is contrary to Islam because this would imply that jihad will not continue until Judgment Day or that there is no eternal hatred between the believers and the unbelievers.[85]

Traditional Islamic treatises on jihad also dealt thoroughly with the taking of booty, an act which is, of course, forbidden by modern international conventions. The Qur'an and hadith have many statements on what constitutes booty and how to divide it equitably among the believers once God has given them victory over the unbelievers.[86] The four schools of fiqh developed elaborate rules to legislate this aspect of jihad, rules and interpretations that have been rejected by the vast majority of Muslims today. The jihadis, on the other hand, argue that these rules are still valid and that booty is, therefore, a lawful part of their war against the West.[87] 'Azzam mentioned that the issue of booty had arisen among the mujahidun in Afghanistan, al-Faraj asserted that those who engaged in jihad against the Egyptian government should be able to seize booty, and a Pakistani jihadi discussed the taking of booty in jihad as if it were a matter of course.[88] Masood Azhar argues that booty is the jihadi's provision from God, since his "livelihood" is under the shade of a spear.[89] Hizb al-Tahrir has even incorporated booty into their proposed constitution for the coming Islamic state, making spoils from warfare one of the central sources of funding for the government.[90] In both declarations of war, bin Ladin mentions booty, stating in 1996 that the blood of American soldiers in Arabia "is permitted [to be spilled] and their wealth is a booty; their wealth is a booty to those who kill them."[91] The 1998 declaration was even more expansive, asserting not only that all Americans—military and civilian— could be killed, but that the mujahidun should "plunder their money wherever and whenever they find it."[92]

There is, finally, the problem of terrorism. Based on one verse in the Qur'an[93] as well as a few ahadith,[94] the jihadis are convinced that creating fear in the hearts of the unbelievers is not only a sound tactic in their war, but one that is supported by Islamic law. Qutb argued that one of the main purposes of jihad was to "strike terror into the hearts of God's enemies who are also the enemies of the advocates of Islam throughout the world, be they open with their hostility and known to the Muslim community, or others who may be discreet with their real feelings, not openly stating their hostile attitude toward Islam."[95] Qutb clearly was advocating the use of terror tactics not just against aggressors or open enemies of his version of Islam, but against anyone who did not support him. Almost every jihadist group affirms a desire to kill or maim men, women, and children in the most horrific ways in order to strike fear in their enemies. Thus Abu Hamza supports suicide bombings not because it is the most efficient way to free occupied Islamic territory, but because "this is the only way the [unbelievers] will be terrorized."[96] As we have seen, bin Ladin himself had ambivalent feelings about the term terrorism, but this should not be confused with his overall conviction about the need to terrorize the enemy. By May 1998 he would state that the terrorism he practiced was commendable because it was directed against the enemies of God—the tyrants and aggressors—and because "terrorizing those and punishing them are necessary measures to straighten things and to make them right."[97] In the 1998 declaration of war terrorism is described as "a legitimate and morally demanded duty," while an al-Qaida statement of 10 October 2001 raises terrorism to a tenet of Islam and the shari'a.[98] Meanwhile, Muhsin al-Awaji, commenting on September 11 and on American condemnation of the attacks, said that "we are proud to be described as terrorizing the enemies of Allah and our enemies."[99]

It is worth reemphasizing that the jihadist commitment to offensive warfare, their belief in terrorizing entire populations, their views on prisoners of war and booty, and their deliberate targeting of innocents have not found widespread support among the vast majority of the Islamic world. This has created a serious problem for the jihadis, for they are depending on a massive uprising of the Muslim community to replace fighters who are killed and to spread their war around the world. The result is that jihadis have been forced to find new grand strategies and military thinking that will deal with the unbelievers while they await the "inevitable" awakening of the umma.

7 *From Mecca to Medina*

We should step back now and examine the daunting task that the jihadis have set for themselves. Not only do they believe that the "attack" by the West and other unbelievers requires a violent response, but by declaring that offensive jihad is lawful, the extremists are in effect stating that the only resolution to their problems they will accept is a world ruled by their version of Islam. They must, therefore, defeat a stunning array of enemies: the West, the Jews, the Christians, the Hindus, the "agent rulers," and any Muslims who do not agree with their form of Islam—the so-called apostates, heretics, and hypocrites. This does not include the ongoing struggle against liberalism, democracy, nationalism, and other ideologies that are also targets for their war. In the absence of an uprising by the entire Islamic world, an event every jihadi fervently hopes will take place soon, extremist groups have had to prioritize their enemies, choosing which each one sees as most dangerous and which must be defeated first before moving on to the next. The result has been what, to the outside observer, might seem like random or even self-defeating attacks, as groups pursue contradictory goals without coordinating strikes with each other.

Yet behind the seeming randomness of the attacks carried out by jihadis are rational strategic choices that have as their basis consistent interpretations of the Qur'an, hadith, and the life of Muhammad. Some of this interpretive work was done by the main ideologues of the jihadist movement, including Ibn Taymiyya and Wahhab as well as al-Banna, Mawdudi, and Qutb. All proffered reasoned arguments about which enemy the true believers must fight and which can be left for the longer-term expansion of Islam, arguments that jihadist groups today have adopted as their own. Ibn Taymiyya, living at a time when the core of the Islamic world had fallen to the Mongols, saw the new rulers as pseudo-Muslims. Their unwillingness to implement the shari'a took them outside the bounds of Islam, he argued, and they therefore had to be removed first, before returning to the offensive jihad against the other unbelievers. Wahhab, on the other hand, directed his violence against the Muslims of his day, arguing that they had become heretics through the adoption of Sufi rituals; by venerating sacred sites, saints, and graves; and other practices, such as celebrating birthdays, that he saw as heterodox. The ideologues of the twentieth century also chose different enemies as the most dangerous. Al-Banna argued that Muslims had to expel the British (and other colonizers) first, liberating all the Islamic lands, and then create a "true" Islamic state that would spread Islam. Mawdudi focused on a larger "revolutionary" war against unbelief and the unbelievers throughout the world. Qutb had perhaps the most detailed strategic vision and one that, as we shall see, would influence later jihadist groups deeply, arguing for a two-pronged attack on both the apostate agent-rulers and the unbelieving "Jewish-Crusaders."

Despite the differences in their arguments, there are a number of concepts that these strategic visions, and their later adaptation by various jihadist groups, share. All the strategies are predicated on the principle that every action carried out in the struggle—including military strategies, priorities for attacks, and the selection of targets—should be inspired by the life of Muhammad and have the support of the Qur'an, hadith, or *sira*.[1] We have looked at how the jihadis view the Qur'an and hadith, as well as some of the ways that they abuse the sacred texts for their own ends. In deciding on which strategies and tactics to use, the jihadis often refer to specific archetypes from these texts to justify their methodologies. The sira are not as well-known by non-Muslims, but they also play an important role in determining the strategies that the jihadis will follow. During the centuries immediately after Muhammad's death the early Muslims not only brought together the sayings that would eventually form the hadith collections, they also wrote several histories of his life, collectively called the sira. These sacralized biographies preserve information and interpretations about Muhammad's calling as both a prophet and political leader that are not in the hadith or the Qur'an. Although not viewed as divine or inerrant by Muslims, the sira, by providing a chronological gloss for the sacred texts, do have a role to play for the Islamic world, showing the actions of Muhammad and the early Muslim state as embedded in human history. The interpretive commentaries added by various authors also give Muslims insight into parts of the Qur'an and Muhammad's actions that are otherwise obscure. Muslims generally read the sira to be inspired by the deeds of Muhammad and to understand how Islam can be applied to their daily lives.

The jihadis have seized on the sira as virtual blueprints for their struggle with the rest of the world. The life of Muhammad becomes the "model for the acquisition and use of power," and the sira therefore must "be studied to produce the defensive and offensive strategies of Islam at every stage of this global confrontation over a very long period of time."[2] The sira, in this reading, show how to carry out Muhammad's "orders," and become as important as the *usul al-fiqh*, a technical legal term in Islamic jurisprudence for the sources of the shari'a—the Qur'an, hadith, analogy, and consensus. This claim gives the sira legislative authority and makes them part of the 'aqida—creed—of Islam.[3] Jihadis are thus convinced that Muslims are obligated to follow whatever the sira show about Muhammad's pronouncements or actions in preaching (da'wa) and jihad, and argue that attempts to denigrate the importance of the sira come from lukewarm Muslims who want to shirk their duty to fight for the supremacy of Islam.[4]

Once again it was Qutb who did much of the early theoretical work on how the course of Muhammad's life should affect the Islamic movement, and jihad in particular. Qutb began with the proposition that Muhammad's mission could be divided into stages, each of which had specific characteristics and goals. This is a common understanding of the life of Muhammad and informs much of Islamic practice, philosophy, and law. Qutb may also have been influenced to think in stages by al-Banna, who divided his movement into three distinct steps as well: "a) Introductory: Disseminating concepts and ideas among the people through oratory and writing, civic action and other practical methods; b) Preparatory: Identifying good and reliable cadre to bear the burden of initiating and sustaining jihad. This is a period of building wisdom among the leaders and military discipline among the recruits. At this stage no one will be admitted to the movement except those willing to carry out their responsibilities in full obedience; c) Execution: The stage of relentless combat and constant effort to achieve the goals. This stage will weed out all but the most honest and sincere, both in their own commitment and in their obedience to the chain of command."[5] Unlike al-Banna, however, Qutb argued that true believers had to take Muhammad alone as their model and see the stages of his mission as not just something that happened in the past, but as eternal archetypes that should shape how a modern Islamic revival would take place. The first stage was Muhammad's time in Mecca, the thirteen years from the beginning of his mission until he migrated to Medina.[6] At Mecca Muhammad was engaged in a peaceful struggle with his unbelieving fellow Arabs, calling them to Islam through reasoned arguments. Qutb noted that he was not allowed to fight or use violence and instead concentrated on winning over a band of dedicated followers, since only a committed vanguard could implement his grand strategic vision. In Qutb's terminology, this stage is one of "building the faith," "grouping, perseverance and steadfastness," and designed to train, educate, and prepare the Muslims for the next stages, which would demand discipline and endurance.

After the believers had been fully grounded in the new faith, Qutb argued that Muhammad deliberately chose to leave Mecca for Medina in order to set up a separate community based on Islamic principles. He also noted that Muhammad attempted to migrate to several other countries and cities before being welcomed by the tribes at Medina, showing that the important point was to locate a safe haven for the Muslims, not to migrate to a specific place. As with most Islamic scholars, Qutb saw this hijra[7] (migration) as an important step in Muhammad's mission. Unlike the vast majority of the ulama, however, he believed that it had continuing significance and should affect the actions of Muslims today.[8]

The next stage came during Muhammad's time in Medina, a period in which an embryonic Islamic state was created. Sections of the Qur'an dealing with a variety of social issues were revealed, and Muhammad began raids on the caravans of those Arab tribes that were hostile to the Muslims. A significant milestone during the Medinan era was the battle of Badr, a victory by the small Islamic community over the powerful Quraysh tribe. Qutb noted that this battle, called by the Qur'an "the criterion," not only distinguished truth from falsehood but also the stage of preparation from the stage of "strength, pre-emption and taking the initiative." In other words, Muhammad was permitted now to engage in offensive warfare against the unbelievers, and the number of Muslims grew exponentially. As the community expanded, Muhammad was able to return to Mecca in triumph, welcomed into this key city without a fight. With Mecca as the center for their new state, the Muslims spread out to engulf an immense amount of territory, from Spain to India, in less than two centuries.

Qutb argued that Muslims of the twentieth century would need to redo these stages in order to experience a true revival of Islam's greatness. As we have seen, he believed that Islam had completely disappeared from the earth and that therefore the modern world was once again steeped in jahiliyya, the ignorance that Muhammad came to replace with Islam. Muslims interested in revival had to recognize that they were faced with the same situation that Muhammad had confronted 1,400 years earlier, and had to start with the basic call (da'wa) to authentic Islam that Muhammad had given. Eventually a number of true believers would form a group (*jama'a*) that would require state power in order to implement the commands of God. At this point, the group, however small it might be, had to follow Muhammad and migrate away from the jahiliyya that surrounded them and set up the kernel of an Islamic state. The most important aspect of the new state, in Qutb's reading of this event, was that it perfectly apply the law of God in both the public and private lives of its citizens. The new state would naturally attract large numbers of admirers who would recognize the power and beauty of Islam, become Muslims, and join the movement, but it would also attract the envy and hatred of the unbelievers, who would attack the believers and have to be repelled by force. At some point (Qutb is unclear exactly when this point would be reached) the Muslims would have to follow Muhammad and go on the offensive, taking the initiative and fighting their enemies physically.

A number of the jihadist groups have accepted Qutb's interpretation of the method of Muhammad to create strategies for action.[9] Over and over the concept of stages appears in jihadist thinking about how to carry out their wars, and, although the precise details vary, the majority include the concepts of "Meccan," "hijra," and "Medinan" phases. Several jihadist ideologues agree that true Islam either no longer exists or has dwindled to just a few believers; that the world is where it was when Muhammad was at Mecca; and that therefore the call (da'wa) to authentic religion must be given anew.[10] Hizb al-Tahrir and affiliated groups argue that da'wa should be in two phases, following their particular interpretation of the sira: a private call that reaches out only to believers, who will form the small vanguard, followed by a public call to Islam for society in general.[11] Hizb al-Tahrir, as well as 'Usama bin Ladin and several prominent theorists, agree with Qutb that the call must coalesce around a group (jama'a) or party (*hizb*).[12] Bin Ladin specifically divided this phase into three: the creation of a group, "hearing," and "obedience."[13] The concept is that the new believers will need careful education into the "true" faith before they can be asked to obey by sacrificing their lives for their beliefs.

The description of this group as a vanguard is telling, because it is a Western (in this case Marxist/Leninist) tactic read back into the life of Muhammad. Mawdudi and Qutb were the theorists most taken with this idea, but later jihadis have also tried to explain what exactly this group will be like, how it will form, and what its purpose will be. Mawdudi's vanguard had to be "fit in spirit and character," fearful of God, and ready to "implicitly follow the law of God without consideration of gain or loss."[14] Both Mawdudi and Qutb believed that the group would face persecution and suffering that would test, refine, and strengthen the vanguard for the coming struggle.[15] Later jihadis have agreed. Based on a few verses in the Qur'an and some marginal hadith, both Abu Hamza and the leaders of al-Muhajiroun argue for the existence of an elite vanguard, "victorious party," or "saved sect," which will establish the order of Allah and carry out jihad despite opposition from others.[16] 'Umar Bakri Muhammad argues that it is, in fact, contrary to Islamic law and practice to work for an Islamic state without such a group.[17] Another jihadi has stated that, based on the believers Muhammad attracted to his side in Mecca, the group will consist primarily of young people, while the elders, parents, and "vested interests" in the various countries will form the opposition to the Muslims, an opposition that will attempt to destroy the group before it can achieve its purpose.[18] Hizb al-Tahrir and other extremists, perhaps inspired by this belief, have specifically targeted universities—especially in non-Islamic countries—for the young activists who will make up the elite vanguard.[19]

Once the true believers have formed a cohesive group, jihadis generally agree that they must make hijra—especially as interpreted by Qutb—in order to follow a legitimate Islamic strategy. Muhammad's migration to Medina is the defining event of Islamic history. Traditional interpreters of the sacred texts, as well as modern Wahhabi scholars, argue that the Qur'an and hadith command other Muslims to migrate, too, but only if they are in an unbelieving country where they are unable to practice their religion freely, or where they are tempted to sin.[20] Modern moderate scholars disagree, using a series of well-attested hadith to maintain that the hijra happened once and will never occur again.[21] The jihadis take a third position, agreeing with the traditional interpreters that migration will continue until the day of judgment, but with an added twist: true Muslims must, at some point, migrate away from their sinful jahili homelands (even if they claim to be Islamic) to a place where an authentic Islamic state can be erected. It is worth emphasizing again that the jihadis have here, as in other instances, declared an innovative interpretation of the texts not supported by either traditional commentators or the majority of modern Islamic scholars.[22]

What is the purpose of this new migration? In his exposition on the necessity for hijra, American jihadi Shamim Siddiqi wrote that it allowed Muslims to gather in one place and to differentiate themselves from the rest of the sinners in the world. It is, indeed, "a culminating point where all the forces fighting for the cause of Allah's [religion] may concentrate at one place to transform themselves into an Islamic state."[23] It would be difficult, he argued, for Muslims to change their own countries from within through some sort of gradual political process. Instead they had to follow Muhammad by separating themselves physically from the ungodliness that surrounds them—even if they remained within the boundaries of the same country—and by creating a pure revolutionary Islamic state.[24] Abu Hamza gave a series of arguments for migration. First he believed it necessary because the very presence of Muslims among the unbelievers aided the infidels, while a failure to join with other Muslims denied the Islamic state any knowledge that the believers might contribute to the cause. He argued as well that living with "homosexuality, . . . usury, drugs, legislators, [polytheists], . . . pagans, . . . crusaders" gave these forbidden things legitimacy, while paying taxes to the infidels helped their unbelief to continue to exist. At the same time, Muslims might become infected with the culture of sin that surrounded them.[25] He also noted, as have other jihadis, that the inability to apply shari'a should in itself be enough to impel Muslims to migrate.[26]

Hizb al-Tahrir has a slightly different approach to the stage of migration, insisting that the important point of the hijra was not a separation from the unbelievers, but Muhammad's search for military and popular support against his enemies. This Hizb al-Tahrir calls "seeking the *nusra* [backing or protection]." In this view, the believing group does not necessarily have to leave its homeland, but should instead be looking for people with power "to open the door for what lies behind them and to secure the popular base." These "powerful people" might include military men or political leaders, but—given the fact that tyrants rule most of the Muslim world—could mean any group that is "important and carr[ies] weight in the Islamic lands."[27] One Hizb al-Tahrir member argues that "we can seek the protection of tribes, military commanders, or the masses as long as they are Muslim. These are classified as styles, which take on many forms and shapes according to the circumstances. Seeking protection from the positions of power does not change but the positions of power themselves may change."[28] The important point was that these men be able to transform the opinions of ordinary Muslims so that they would come over to the side of the vanguard and support them in the next phase of the struggle. Another way of seeing the hijra is thus as a transfer of power into the hands of Muhammad so that he was able to arrive at Medina and immediately set up the first Islamic state.[29] Hizb al-Tahrir is actively pursuing this phase of the "method of Muhammad," and is looking for any influential groups, in any country, to transfer power into their hands so that the party can create a true Islamic state and begin the jihad against the unbelievers.[30]

Like Hizb al-Tahrir, jihadis in general are not committed to any particular country, territory, or even part of the earth as the focus for their hijra and state. The one commonality is that it be Islamic land, but even this is not a unanimous opinion. Siddiqi thought that parts of America could even become Islamic territory and thus the object of hijra. He advocated using the electoral process to take over one of the fifty states peacefully, implementing shari'a there and making it the envy of its neighboring states. Americans would be attracted to the social justice created in this small Islamic land and would vote to establish shari'a in their own states. Over time the entire country would become part of the umma, and the Islamic state would naturally arise on American territory. He also argued that "if an Islamic Movement anywhere in this world succeeds in establishing Allah's Deen within its sovereign rights, it would be the homeland for all the Muslims of the world. Muslims, anywhere in this world, would have the right to migrate to that Islamic State and obtain its citizenship. The Islamic State may, however, direct the Muslims of the world to stay where they are and struggle for the establishment of Allah's Deen with her moral and ideological support."[31] Siddiqi thus envisages the true believers acting as subversive cells behind enemy lines in support of the Islamic state. Other jihadis have similar conceptions of how the migration and Islamic state will take shape. Shukri Ahmad Mustafa, an Egyptian jihadi who assassinated a high Egyptian official, belonged to a jihadist group that argued for Muslims to withdraw from their own jahili societies and create a distinct Islamic state within their own territories, rather than migrating to a distant land.[32] 'Umar Bakri Mohammad, on the other hand, first moved from Egypt to Saudi Arabia and then to England, and has attempted to create a state-within-a-state in Britain. The name of his group, al-Muhajiroun [the migrants], shows his dedication to the principle of migration without making any statement about where or how the hijra will take place.

The victory of the Taliban in Afghanistan convinced several jihadist groups that here, at last, was the true Islamic state that required their migration. Abu Hamza and his group, Supporters of Shari'ah, held a conference not long after the Taliban came to power to urge Muslims in Britain to migrate to Afghanistan— the state that had "returned Islam."[33] He also recommended that Muslims "divest themselves from the west. The Muslims should stop paying any taxes, sell off their property, withdraw their money from all banks, quit their work, left [*sic*] immediately," and either migrate to Afghanistan or start to fight.[34] At about the same time bin Ladin referred to Afghanistan as "the only country in the world today that has the Shari'a," arguing therefore that "it is compulsory upon all the Muslims all over the world to help Afghanistan. And to make hijra to this land, because it is from this land that we will dispatch our armies all over the world to smash the [unbelievers] all over the world (and spread Al-Islam)." [35] It is significant that bin Ladin always referred to Mullah Omar as "'Amir al-Mu'minin" (Commander of the Faithful), a title reserved for the Caliph alone,[36] and that he specifically compared Afghanistan to Medina on at least one occasion.[37] After the United States defeated the Taliban in the fall of 2001, bin Ladin stopped calling for migration to a particular place, although he remained insistent that hijra was absolutely necessary and was tied to jihad.[38]

This is consistent with other jihadis' beliefs that hijra, whatever land is its focus, must be followed by a Medinan phase. During this stage the Islamic state (called *Khilafa* [Caliphate] by the jihadis) either already exists or is now created by the migrants themselves, and the Muslims immediately begin a phase of open warfare with the unbelievers. Jihadis argue that Muhammad set up an Islamic state as soon as he migrated to Medina, showing the importance for the furtherance of both his mission (and their own) of placing territory under the control of the true believers.[39] A belief in the significance of territorial control is one explanation for why many jihadis argue that Islam ceased to exist with the dismantling of the Ottoman Caliphate in 1924 and why they believe that it will revive only when a true Islamic state has physical control over land. Kalim Siddiqui argues that it is not enough to have an Islamic party win elections in one nation and then declare that the country to be the Khilafa. He viewed this as a form of nationalism, an infidel concept, one that was unfit for the basis of the true Islamic state.[40] Rather, for Khilafa to arise, total authority[41] and power must be in the hands of authentic believers, they then must set up a true Islamic state, and the new state must perfectly apply the shari'a.[42] There can be no sharing of power with other political parties nor the opportunity for the next election to strip control over the country from the hands of the believers. In some jihadist readings of the Khilafa it is not even necessary for an entire nation to be under the control of the believers; a sizable piece of land is enough.

While many jihadis do not care about the details of the future Islamic state, a few jihadist groups have attempted to outline the shape that their utopia will take. Hizb al-Tahrir, the group that has done the most theoretical work on the Khilafa, produced a constitution for their ideal state that envisions a totalitarian dictatorship without a legislature or formal judiciary that could check the unchallenged power of the ruler. Private behavior—and even secret thoughts—would be regulated by the state, ensuring that everyone supported completely the version of Islam defined by Hizb al-Tahrir.[43] A large number of jihadis believe that the only foreign policy of the Khilafa would be to convey Islam to the rest of the world through jihad and da'wa, an eternal struggle with the unbelievers through word or combat that will never acknowledge borders or boundaries to the state's expansion.[44] The general tenor of jihadist writing shows that they believe the Khilafa will solve all the problems of the Islamic world—economic, military, political, social, and cultural—without any detailed plans or programs. As a jihadi put it in a lecture, once the Khilafa has appeared God will grant the true Muslims "the authority to pledge the allegiance to one [Caliph], upon hearing and obeying in the pleasant and unpleasant, the difficult and the easy, to rule by the Book of Allah . . . and the sunna of His Messenger. . . . This will lead to the annexation of the rest of the countries in the Islamic world, as they would soon merge into a single Khilafa state. Then it will carry the banner of Islam as a message of guidance and light to the rest of the world. At the same time, the Muslims will hope that Allah . . . will exchange for them security after their fear, by making them strong materially, spiritually and in purpose. Then eliminating the dread of the disbelievers and their superpowers from Muslim souls. . . . The direction of the wind will blow in the favor of the umma against the will of their opponents."[45] There is only one explanation for the conviction that the Khilafa will end all the problems of the Islamic world: this is what the sira tells them about the life of Muhammad, and, if they follow his example, they too can expect to be blessed with success.

Despite agreement about this very general outline for the creation and form of the Khilafa, one central dispute remains: is it

possible to engage in offensive jihad without the official establishment of the Islamic state? Jihadist groups agree that there is
no need for a Caliph or an Islamic state to begin a *defensive* jihad.
Thus Ayman al-Zawahri, one of the leaders of Egyptian Islamic
Jihad and a top member of al-Qaida, said in an interview that Islamic territory had been occupied for eighty years and had to be
liberated through jihad now, rather than waiting until some theoretical "preparation" stage had been passed.[46] There are also
a few prominent groups who have argued that even offensive
jihad—taking the battle to the unbelievers rather than waiting to
be attacked—must begin without the Khilafa.[47] Bin Ladin might
be classed as one of these, since he has argued that Muslims need
to wage jihad to create the Khilafa itself, rather than first setting
up the state and then declaring war.[48] 'Abdullah 'Azzam discussed several stages after hijra, culminating in jihad, but he did
not believe that the formation of an Islamic state was a necessary
preliminary step.[49] 'Umar Bakri Mohammad takes a different
position, arguing that Islamic law will not permit a jihad directed
against fellow Muslims to set up the Khilafa.[50] His ideas can be
compared to those of Hizb al-Tahrir, the most prominent supporters of the need for an Islamic state.[51] As a group, Hizb al-
Tahrir is firmly committed to the idea that only the Caliph can
declare offensive war against the infidels, and a Caliph will appear and be recognized only when he sets up the Khilafa. Several
arrested Hizb al-Tahrir members have disputed their convictions
for inciting violence by stating that they are following the

"method of Muhammad" and—like him—would never engage in jihad without an Islamic state.[52] To support their argument that several stages remain before offensive jihad can be declared, Hizb al-Tahrir members also point to the fact that the nusra has not yet been sought. Yet Hizb al-Tahrir is committed to *defensive* jihad—broadly defined—and has encouraged attacks on the United States in Afghanistan and Iraq and war by Muslims in Kashmir, Chechnya, and other hotspots around the globe. As we shall see, they also envision a defensive jihad aimed at overthrowing the "apostate" rulers of the Islamic lands, a jihad that might lead directly to the creation of the Khilafa.[53]

This discussion shows that jihadist groups concur that the Islamic movement must follow Muhammad through stages that include a peaceful time of preparation, a migration, the creation of an Islamic state, and finally open warfare, although there is no accord over the timing or precise shape of these stages. There is even less agreement on the focus of either the defensive or offensive jihads that the final stage of their strategic vision requires. Which of their many enemies should they attack first? What sorts of military strategies should they follow? And what objectives should they specifically attack—financial, economic, military, civilian, or religious targets? Most of the contradictory statements and attacks that have confused observers over the past few years are due to the disparate answers to these questions that jihadist groups have settled on. Yet even here there is more harmony than might appear at first glance. There are, for instance, only two jihadist views about which enemy should be given priority, encapsulated in the phrases "the greater unbelief first, then the lesser unbelief" and "the near enemy first, then the far enemy." The first of these ideas follows the work of Ibn Taymiyya, and especially his declaration that the "people of Islam should join forces and support each other to get rid of the main [greater] '[unbelief]' who is controlling the countries of the Islamic world."[54] In Ibn Taymiyya's day, the greater unbelief was the Mongols, who controlled the heartland of the Islamic lands and claimed to be Muslims but who, in Taymiyya's view, were actually unbelievers. Ibn Taymiyya contended that these unjust occupiers had to be defeated before the Muslims could take on the other enemies of true Islam (like foreign infidels). 'Usama bin Ladin and al-Qaida in general have maintained that the main unbelief today is the United States: the force that stands behind the lesser unbelief of the apostate rulers, controlling them and using them for its own ends. Once the puppet master is destroyed, the downfall of the tyrants will inevitably follow. Throughout the past decade, bin Ladin and his supporters have had a running argument with other jihadis, trying to convince them not to be distracted by other tempting targets, but to focus their energy on the United States alone until the main enemy is defeated.[55] The variety of attacks carried on around the world suggest that al-Qaida has so far been unsuccessful in winning over all jihadis to their strategic vision, although there have been expressions of support for the United States as the main enemy from some.[56]

This is almost certainly because other jihadist groups prioritize attacking the "near enemy" before taking on the "far enemy," a prescription that comes directly from the Qur'an.[57] The problem is that the notion of a "near enemy" has several possible interpretations. One sees them as the non-Muslims that have invaded Islamic lands, while another argues that the unjust rulers are the near enemy, who must be overthrown and replaced with a righteous Caliph. It is also possible that a few groups see this enemy as the "heretics" within Islamic countries. Bin Ladin, perhaps again trying to win over other jihadis to his strategy, has adopted the first interpretation.[58] The presence of U.S. forces in various Islamic countries (including Arabia), as well as the U.S. intervention in Iraq (even in 1991), Somalia, and elsewhere has allowed bin Ladin to collapse the two formulations of the primary enemy into one: the United States becomes both the greater unbelief *and* the near enemy.[59] Other jihadist groups have chosen to see the occupiers as the unbelievers who happen to be in their particular part of the Islamic world (for a given definition of "occupier.") Thus in Pakistan, the near enemy is India, which holds Kashmir and other territory claimed by the jihadis; in the Caucasus it is Russia which occupies Chechnya, Ingushetia, and nearby Islamic lands; in Palestine, Jordan, and the Middle East in general it becomes Israel or the Christians in Lebanon; in Egypt and Algeria certain jihadist groups have chosen to see native Christians (like the Copts) or tourists as unbelieving forces that must be attacked.[60]

This view of the near enemy is not the only one. Jihadis who disagree with bin Ladin have used various sources—especially Ibn Taymiyya and assorted ahadith—to argue that the agent-rulers are the worst of the near enemies and that therefore they must be fought and killed even before taking on the United States, Israel, or the remaining West.[61] In Ibn Taymiyya's words they were the "most evil of peoples amongst Allah's creation," because not only do they refuse to follow God's laws themselves, but they also prevent other Muslims from doing the same.[62] Abu Hamza has made a similar argument for targeting the "apostates," and praises those groups, like GIA and the Algerian Salafist Group for Da'wa and Fighting, that have directly attacked their "sinful" political leaders.[63] The firmest supporters of focusing the attack on the "agent-rulers" are the members of Hizb al-Tahrir.[64] In their view, bin Ladin has it exactly backward: the best way to stop the United States is by liberating the Islamic world from the "gang of agent rulers." The United States will then be powerless to carry out any evil plots against Islam, since it will no longer have mindless puppets to do its will.[65] The 2003 war with Iraq, in Hizb al-Tahrir's opinion, demonstrates this point perfectly. The United States would not have been able to wage its unjust war without the aid of neighboring Islamic rulers, who have thus through their actions declared their own infidelity.[66] In the same way, Hizb al-Tahrir believes that the best method for driving out the occupiers from Islamic lands is to remove the leaders who refuse to prosecute war vigorously against the unbelievers in their midst. They argue specifically that Israel would have been destroyed long ago if the Islamic leaders in the states that surrounded the Jewish state had truly wanted to do so.[67] Like Ibn Taymiyya, Hizb al-Tahrir also justifies killing the leaders of Islamic countries because of their refusal to implement the laws of God. In one particularly chilling document, the group argues that this is such an important matter that it will necessitate the killing not only of the agent rulers, but also of all those who have supported them in any way, either actively or passively, "even if this led to several years of fighting and even if it led to the killing of millions of Muslims and to the martyrdom of millions of believers."[68] Note the distinction here between "Muslims,"—those who have made the confession of faith with their mouths but who have not lived it out with their lives—and the "believers," who support their confession with their actions.

A final reading of the "near enemy" finds them in the "heretics" such as the Shi'a or Ahmadis, or in any ordinary Muslims who refuse to pray or follow all the commandments of God. They are described by some jihadis as the worst enemies of Islam and therefore are to be fought and killed even before attacking the United States or other Western enemies.[69] This vision of the near enemy comes from Ibn Taymiyya and Wahhab, who argued for a war against any Muslims who refused to pay alms or pray in the prescribed manner.[70] Hizb al-Tahrir puts a jihad against these "apostates" on the same level as their struggle with the agent-rulers, and has threatened to kill them all, even if this means the death of millions of "so-called" Muslims.[71] Abu Musab al-Zarqawi's decision to kill Iraqi Shi'a first and then attack the occupying Americans was not an afterthought nor did it show his group's lack of discipline, but rather it was based on his calculated belief that the Shi'a were the most evil of people and that they needed therefore to be thrown "into hell."[72] Attacks by jihadis on "heretics" or "apostates" in places as far removed as Saudi Arabia, Iraq, and Pakistan reflect this interpretation of the closest unbelievers.

Selection of the main enemy is important for the jihadist war, but it is only the first step in constructing their strategic vision. They have also chosen specific targets, at times through a pragmatic reading of their enemy's weaknesses, but also by once again turning to the sacred texts as well as to the sira of Muhammad. The decision to attack Madrid's train system just before an election, for instance, demonstrated a willingness by these particular jihadis to focus their strategy on political manipulation, rather than on simply killing as many of the infidels as possible. The note claiming responsibility for the attack made it clear, however, that the jihadis viewed this attack as part of the larger war to regain "Islamic" lands for the umma.[73] This interpretation is supported by the discovery of subsequent planned attacks (one disrupted in April and the other in October 2004). Other jihadis have shown much less understanding of the complexities of the enemies that they face. 'Usama bin Ladin believed that the attacks on symbols of liberalism and military power in New York and Washington would frighten the United States into a withdrawal from Islamic lands, just as previous administrations had been persuaded to abandon Lebanon and Somalia by spectacular strikes. Meanwhile, Mufti Khubiab Sahib has argued that all the "anti-Islam" forces share one important weakness: a reliance upon a few individuals. "This personality worshipping epidemic is the greatest weakness of the enemy," he writes. "Thus to break the enemy's Anti-Islam resolve, a plan to remove these warlords from the scene, would offer untold advantages to the Mujahideen. Once the enemy's leading lights disappear from the scene, the whole nation becomes a rudderless ship." Khubiab suggests as well that polytheists and Jews have different psychologies that require a focus on different targets. The polytheists—Hindus— he wrote, respond only to attacks on their wealth and will do anything possible to preserve their worldly possessions. The Jews, on the other hand, do not care about money, but they will sacrifice everything in order to save their lives. The correct strategy, then, is to attack the economic objectives of the polytheists and the manpower of the Jews.[74] Masood Azhar, meanwhile, cites various ahadith to argue that the most efficacious targets are the wealth and economy of the infidels.[75] A bin Ladin statement, in which he argues for a form of attrition warfare directed at the economy of the United States, may show that he now agrees with this view.[76]

The jihadis have prioritized their enemies, selected their targets, and decided to go to war. Throughout the seventies, eighties, and nineties dozens of different groups used their strategies to attack Muslims who disagreed with them, Israel, the United States, India, Jews, Christians, Hindus, and others. Al-Qaida is but the latest in a long line of jihadist groups that believes it understands how to revive the Islamic umma and return their community to greatness. One problem yet remains: prosecuting the war itself has not gone as easily as they believed it would, and it has been exceedingly difficult to turn theory into practice.

8 *Jihadist Ideology and the War on Terror*

Theory

It should now be obvious why the United States had to be attacked on September 11. Inspired by their distinctive ideology, certain extremists decided that the United States had to be destroyed. There are two central innovations in the ideology that allow—even demand—the destruction of the United States and the murder of thousands of innocents: an aberrant definition of tawhid, and a concentration on violence as the core of their religion. Unlike the vast majority of the Islamic world, the extremists give tawhid political implications and use it to justify all their violent acts. They assert that tawhid means God alone has sovereignty and His laws alone—as laid out in the Qur'an and hadith and by certain traditional jurists—are normative. Thus the only acceptable society for the jihadis is a government that applies the tenets of Islamic law in a way that they believe is correct. Based on this definition of tawhid, the extremists argue that democracy, liberalism, human rights, personal freedom, international law, and international institutions are illegal, illegitimate, and sinful. Because it grants sovereignty to the people and allows them to make laws for their society rather than depending entirely on the God-given legal system of Islam, democracy is the focus for jihadist critiques. The United States is recognized by the jihadis as the center of liberalism and democracy, a center that is willing to spread its ideas and challenge other ways of organizing society, and thus must be destroyed along with democracy itself. The antidemocratic rhetoric of Zarqawi and bin Ladin is not, then, just a reaction to U.S. policies, but rather a reflection of their own most deeply held religio-political views of the world.

Violence also permeates jihadist thought. In their reading of history, the conflict between the United States and Islam is part of a universal struggle between good and evil, truth and falsehood, belief and infidelity, that began with the first human beings and will continue until the end of time. A literal clash of civilizations is taking place around the world and, in the end, only one system can survive: Muslims must rid the earth of democracy or else the supporters of democracy (especially the United States, but the entire "West" as well) will destroy true Islam. Jihadis do not believe that this is a theoretical or ideological struggle that can be played out peacefully; rather, the existence of a political or legal system with provisions that transgress the bounds of the shari'a is an act of aggression against Islam that must be dealt with through revolutionary force.

Because history is dominated by the struggle between good and evil, jihadis assert that all Muslims are called by God to participate in the fight—physically if at all possible, or at least by word or financially—acting as God's sword on earth to deal with the evildoers and their wicked way of life. Muslims who answer the call to fight must do so solely to win God's pleasure so that, in the end, it does not matter if the holy warrior accomplishes anything positive through his violence and incitement to violence: intentions alone count. If a *mujahid* is killed while slaughtering innocent civilians or soldiers on the field of battle, and he acted with pure intentions, he will be guaranteed a welcome into a paradise of unimaginable delights. At the end of time the jihadis envision a world ruled solely by their version of Islam, a world in which "the religion will be for God alone." Thus the jihadis believe that they are more than small groups of violent people who have murdered thousands of men, women, and children. Instead they are honored participants in a cosmic drama, one that will decide the fate of the world and that will ultimately end with the victory of the good, the virtuous, and the true believers.

In addition to fighting evil for God's pleasure, al-Qaida had more mundane short and long-term objectives for the 9/11 assault, objectives that have been articulated by its leaders and that they have lived out. In the short term, al-Qaida wanted to energize a war effort that they began during the early nineties, convince a larger number of Muslims to join their cause, and frighten the United States into leaving all Islamic lands. Al-Qaida's longer term goals included converting all Muslims to their version of Islam, expanding the only legitimate Islamic state (Afghanistan) until it contained any lands that had ever been ruled by Islamic law, and, finally, taking the war beyond the borders of even this expansive state until the entire world was ruled by their extremist Islam. In pursuit of these ends, they believed that the murder of thousands of innocent civilians—including Muslims—was not only legally justified but commanded by God Himself. The jihadist war is thus, in many ways, a struggle over who will control the future of Islam: will this ancient religion become associated with the hatred and violence of the jihadis, or the more tolerant vision proposed by moderate, liberal, and traditional Muslims?

Practice

Yet al-Qaida failed to achieve two of their short-term goals on September 11. The greater Islamic world did not rise, take up the sword, and join their cause, while the United States decided to become more involved in Islamic lands rather than retreating behind its borders. Both of these developments have created dilemmas for the leaders of al-Qaida and allied groups, although the reaction (or lack thereof) of the vast majority of the Islamic world has been the greater blow. Everything that 'Usama bin

Ladin and other jihadis have hoped to achieve depends upon re-cruiting new mujahidun and expanding the war. Since 9/11, ji-hadis have established a theoretical explanation for this seminal failure by returning to their ideological roots—particularly the works of Sayyid Qutb and their views of history as a series of rep-etitious events. There are several templates that bin Ladin and other extremists use to understand the current conflict—the struggle against Pharaoh (the archetypical tyrant), the Mongol conquest, and the eternal battle of good and evil—but the most important template, and the one to which the jihadis always re-turn, is the war against the crusaders. Jihadist discussions of these Western incursions have always talked about the aggression committed against the Islamic world, but since the war in Af-ghanistan the emphasis has changed to the response of the Is-lamic world to the crusader offensive: confused, erratic, and lacking unity. The result was a series of wars that lasted for cen-turies and included serious defeats for the believers. Jihadis have therefore argued that their supporters should not be discouraged by the lack of a mass uprising by the umma, and should instead have the perseverance, patience, and unity commanded by God. This is a war that could last two hundred years, but eventually Islam will produce another Salah al-Din who will rouse the Is-lamic world, unite the Muslims against their enemies, and drive them from the lands of their community.[1]

But there is another jihadist explanation for the apathy of the greater Islamic world to their cause: they believe that they alone are the true believers. They disparage any Muslims who will not participate in their jihad as "sinners" or "hypocrites," or at the very least think of them as sheep who have been led astray by evil ulama and the tyrant rulers. The apathy of the Islamic world to their cause is thus only to be expected. Sayyid Qutb took a much harder line. As we have seen, in his exegesis on the Qur'an as well as in his other writings, he argued that the world had lapsed into the ignorance that had characterized society before Muhammad began his mission. Qutb thus believed that Islam no longer existed, and that all those who declared themselves Muslims were deluding themselves about their true status: they would be real Muslims only when the laws of Islam were put into force in an Islamic society. He even called those Muslims who borrowed laws, morals, and ideas about how to organize society from the West "worse than unbelievers."[2] The result of this line of thinking was a declaration that any territory without Islamic legal provisions— whether the population thought of itself as Muslim or not—was part of the "House of War," and that therefore "neither their lives nor their properties are protected."[3] During the seventies and eighties, a few extremist groups took Qutb's argument to mean that any Muslim who did not strive to implement the laws of Islam through jihad were unbelievers, and therefore made it licit to spill their blood and take their property.[4] Most current jihadist groups do not go this far, but they have adopted certain practices during the war on terror which border on this takfiri attitude. In the first place, they are certainly willing to risk the deaths of innocent Muslims by using weapons that cannot discriminate between soldiers and civilians, and by attacking their enemies in public places frequented by noncombatants. Secondly, jihadis such as Abu Musab al-Zarqawi, as well as clerics in Saudi Arabia, have repeatedly declared takfir on entire groups of Muslims (such as anyone who helps the Americans in Iraq, anyone who voted in the Iraqi elections, anyone who helps the Iraqi government, etc.) and have purposely targeted these civilians.[5]

This attitude has created a dilemma for the jihadis. They understand that they must appeal to ordinary Muslims to join their cause if they are going to win their lengthy war against the "crusaders and Jews." Yet, at the same time, they believe that ideological and religious purity is necessary for their cause, and this purity demands that they regard as enemies any Muslims who do not actively support them. Different jihadist groups have dealt with this dilemma in various ways. The most common response is to attempt to win over Muslims to their cause through da'wa:[6] calling ordinary Muslims "back" to true Islam. Like Wahhab, the extremists have decided that they should direct the majority of their missionary activity at erring Muslims and not at the unbelieving world. The result has been a concentration on preaching the jihadist version of Islam to Muslims in extremist mosques as well as through Internet sites, magazines, pamphlets, and privately published books, all directed at converting fellow Muslims to their way of thinking and acting.

Al-Qaida also failed to achieve a second short-term goal: convincing the United States to leave Islamic lands and the Arabian peninsula in particular. This was a surprise to 'Usama bin Ladin and the other leaders of al-Qaida, who did not foresee the decision by the United States to engage the jihadis and their supporters in Afghanistan. In his statements about the United States before 9/11, bin Ladin emphasized past American decisions to retreat from countries after determined attacks by terrorists. The U.S. response after the explosion that killed 241 marines in Beirut and the "Black Hawk down" incident in Mogadishu are often mentioned in his statements as proof that the United States is cowardly and not prepared for a long conflict.[7] In 1998 he would say in an interview, "We have seen in the last decade the decline of the American government and the weakness of the American soldier who is ready to wage Cold Wars and unprepared to fight long wars. This was proven in Beirut when the Marines fled after two explosions. It also proves they can run in less than 24 hours, and this was also repeated in Somalia."[8] Bin Ladin anticipated that the United States would react to another blow like Beirut or Somalia by fulfilling one of his seminal demands: to leave the military bases in Riyadh and Khobar and perhaps to abandon altogether the rest of the Arabian peninsula. The collapse of Afghanistan, seen by bin Ladin as the only true Islamic state and the land that he designated for hijra, has also been distressing, although jihadis see this as a possible opportunity to draw the United States into a lengthy war for which it is ill-suited.[9]

As with the problem of inciting jihad among ordinary Muslims, bin Ladin has found solace for the failure of his strategies in the example of the crusades. A thousand years ago the Europeans also seemed invincible, and numerous attempts to drive them from the Levant failed miserably. The new crusader assault is equally fearsome, but it too will eventually be repelled. Bin Ladin points as well to the steadfastness of the young Islamic community in its confrontation with the Persian empire to argue that this modern superpower, composed of the "most cowardly of people," can be defeated by the umma.[10] He, and other jihadis, also emphasize a more recent historical example to show that the Islamic nation has nothing to fear from the United States: the defeat of the Soviet Union in Afghanistan. According to jihadist mythology, it was the mujahidun, working entirely on their own, who defeated the Soviet army and thus caused the entire Soviet empire to collapse. Unlike his impressions of the United States, bin Ladin thought the Soviets a fearsome enemy, one that required ten years of concerted effort to defeat. The most important lesson that he drew from his years as a mujahidun in Afghanistan: that even a small number of determined Islamic warriors could explode the myth of a "superpower" and bring the toughest seeming opponent to its knees.[11]

Thus, despite the failure of at least part of his strategy, bin Ladin—and other jihadis—have been undeterred. The successes of the war in Afghanistan and Iraq, including the recent elections, have not convinced them that they have been defeated, and they have determined to fight on.

Response

How, then, should the world respond to the jihadis and their revolutionary ideology? As should be obvious from this discussion, the extremists themselves are not interested in dialogue, compromise, or participation in a political process to attain their ends. For ideological reasons, they have chosen to use violence rather than peaceful means to resolve their problems and achieve their objectives. The ultimate goals of the jihadis are likewise so radical—to force the rest of the world to live under their version of Islamic law—that there is no way to agree to them without sacrificing every other society on the planet. The United States and other countries must then find reasonable strategies that will exploit the failures of the jihadis, stop the extremists from carrying out violent attacks, minimize the appeal of their beliefs, and eventually end their war with the world.

A complete detailing of the strategies necessary to defeat the jihadis is beyond the scope of this book; however, it is possible to present schematically the overall national and international policy that will be necessary to meet their challenge. The significant difference between the ideas presented here and other proposals for fighting the war on terror is the conclusion drawn from the preceding discussion: that the center of the jihadist movement is its ideology, which must be directly confronted, challenged, and defeated. At the same time, the near term threat to non-jihadist lives cannot be ignored. This implies a two-track approach, one ideological and the other physical. The anti-jihadist strategy will also need to consider short- and long-term policies, keeping in mind objectives for each stage of the struggle that will meet the theory and flawed practice of the jihadis.

The most important short-term objective is to stop the jihadis from killing more people, and especially to prevent them from carrying out another attack on the scale of September 11. This is the only objective that involves the military or law enforcement, and of course the military in particular should be used as sparingly as possible. Since the jihadis have chosen to fight their war asymmetrically, the general tactics to follow are those used with any insurgency: taking away land, time, and funding from the jihadis. The campaign in Afghanistan is an example of taking away land—making certain that the extremists do not have territory under their control that they can use as bases for organizing attacks against the United States and other enemies. Since they believe that they must have land under their direct control, land where their version of the shari'a can be applied, expelling the jihadis from territory also attacks their ideology. To take away time requires that the military or law enforcement officials press the jihadis simultaneously around the world. This has been the policy of the U.S. government since 9/11, and the result has been to prevent the extremists from having the time that they need to plan new offensives. It has also moved the battlefield from inside the United States to other countries, where the enemy can be fought on American terms, with soldiers rather than civilians, and with the help of international coalitions.[12] Finally, the jihadis will be able to kill large numbers of unbelievers and innocent Muslims only if they have the money to buy explosives or sophisticated weapons, or to pay for training terrorist cells. The attempts to freeze funding for the extremists through international controls on money transfers and "charitable" foundations is part of the effort to prevent the jihadis from paying for more serious weapons than grenade launchers and suicide bombings.[13] All of these efforts presuppose the involvement of not just the United States, but as many countries as possible in the simultaneous suppression of extremist groups around the world. International diplomacy, then, naturally takes on special significance throughout the entire course of the anti-jihadist grand strategy.

Military or law enforcement efforts are just part of the short-term strategy. Countering the extremist preaching (or da'wa) that the jihadis use to recruit members and win support or sympathy in the wider Islamic world is equally important and not just for the short term, but also for the longer effort. As in any war, jihadis must replace fighters lost in battle in order to continue their offensive and to spread their beliefs throughout the Islamic world. They are also, as we have seen, determined to convert the rest of the Muslims to their beliefs, and various groups have expanded great efforts to reach out to Muslims in the Islamic world, Europe, and the United States.[14] The method that jihadis have chosen to call their recruiting, da'wa, allows them to subvert an Islamically acceptable concept and to take over mosques around the world for their own purposes. As a report by Freedom House shows, preaching of the violent concepts that underlie the jihadist ideology are not just confined to specific radical mosques, but are also commonly taught in Wahhabi Islamic centers in the United States and elsewhere.[15] The expulsions of extremist imams in France, Spain, and Britain that have taken place since 9/11 are one method for dealing with jihadist da'wa, but it is also necessary to work with moderate and liberal Muslims to prevent extremists from taking over mosques and to help them in educating their youth to differentiate their religion from that of the fanatics.[16] Muslims need, for instance, to understand the implications of the jihadist definition of tawhid and the extremist focus on violence, but even more than this they need to see that the jihadis view all other Muslims as lesser believers who can be killed at will in the war with the unbelievers.

A third aspect of the short-term struggle is to take away the single best recruiting tool that the jihadis possess: the Palestinian-Israeli conflict. Many jihadis, including bin Ladin and Ayman al-Zawahri, believe that there is no difference between the Jews and the "crusaders," and that the two are acting in concert to destroy Islam.[17] The Palestinian-Israeli conflict is thus sacralized and made part of the worldwide battle between truth and falsehood.[18] Al-Qaida has, however, decided that they must focus on attacking Americans and the United States, since the expulsion of the United States from Islamic lands will lead to the destruction of Israel, while destroying Israel will not be enough to win the overall war with "falsehood."[19] Yet while al-Qaida and other jihadis have left the actual fighting in Palestine to specific organizations like Hamas, they have not been backward about exploiting the concern for the Palestinian cause in the wider Islamic world to gain sympathy and support for their own jihad.[20] An equitable solution to the Palestinian-Israeli conflict, and especially one that leads to a recognition of the right of Israel to exist side by side with an independent Palestinian state, will therefore not stop the violence from al-Qaida and similarly minded jihadist groups, but such a solution will deprive these extremists of a valuable means for winning new recruits and make it more difficult for them to replace fighters lost in battle. Of course, to say that this is a desirable goal will not make it any easier to find a solution to this seemingly intractable problem, but it is worth pointing out that, in addition to peace and justice, there are other reasons to work toward a fair resolution to the conflict.

Finally, perhaps the simplest way to prevent the jihadis from garnering sympathy and support from other Muslims is to stigmatize the extremists and their war. There are many ways to do this, but one easy method is to change the names of both the war on terror and the enemy. This is not something that the United States can do on its own, but rather such changes must be advanced in cooperation with other nations, and with the Islamic world in particular. The term "war on terror" has never been satisfactory because it suggests that this is war against a tactic, that there is no agency (or enemy), and that it will be difficult if not impossible to know when the war is won. Changing the name of the war to something like "the war on jihadis" or "the war on jihadism," will differentiate the extremists from other Muslims, give the war an enemy with a definite ideology and objectives, and suggest that there is an end point to work toward. Another naming suggestion for the conflict is the "war on the *khawarij.*" The khawarij were heterodox Muslims who appeared soon after the death of Muhammad to claim that they alone were true believers: all the other "so-called" Muslims were in fact apostates who had to be fought and killed. The similarities between these beliefs and those of the takfir-declaring jihadis have been commented on by other Muslims, and the accusation by Muslim experts that the jihadis are khawarij is common enough that the extremists have felt compelled to deny that they are anything like these "heretics." Of course, the United States cannot call the jihadis heterodox, but it can encourage the Islamic world to use a designation that is already present in Islamic polemics against the extremists. Making khawarij a common term for the jihadis will not only differentiate them from the rest of the Islamic world, but it will also make it plain to moderate Muslims just how heterodox and violent toward other Muslims the jihadis are.

These short-term strategies, necessary as they are, will deal with only some of the jihadist challenge. For instance, keeping radical imams and jihadist preachers from mosques will not stop them from making their arguments through the Internet, private publishing houses, or in person. The world's response to 9/11 needs to include longer-term methods that permanently prevent the jihadis from winning the hearts and minds of Muslims. Most particularly, something must be done about the deeper underlying issues in Islamic countries, and especially in the Arab Middle East—problems such as tyrannical governments, corruption, and economic backwardness—that have made at least some Muslims willing to give the jihadis a hearing. Any longer term strategy must, however, do more than deal with these issues: it must also counter directly the specific arguments made by the jihadis through their ideology. A grand strategy that did not take this into consideration could succeed in the short run but fail over time, since the jihadist argument is that economic or political success in this world means nothing.

Fortunately, there is a particular approach that answers both of these demands by taking on the central focus of the jihadist ideology and providing a solution as well to an underlying cause of their appeal to the rest of the Islamic world. As many experts have pointed out, the extremists have gained support because of widespread discontent with the oppressive governments that dominate the Arab and Muslim world as well as the stagnant economic conditions that reign in that part of the globe. There has been a long-standing debate over how best to prevent terrorist attacks and limit the appeal of groups like the jihadis, with some experts citing economic development as the main cure for violence,[21] while others argue that greater freedom, which gives ordinary citizens peaceful ways to resolve their problems, will gradually end the appeal of the extremist groups.[22] Only democratization, however, will directly attack the jihadist ideology while creating governments that are more responsive to their citizens. The jihadist argument is that democracy is completely antithetical to Islam and moreover is specifically designed to destroy the religion. If democracies can flourish in Islamic lands without disturbing the practices and beliefs of Islam, the entire jihadist argument will collapse. While there are many reasons to hope and work for democracies in the Middle East—that they might end despotic regimes, create the conditions for economic development, end oppression and corruption, and so on—the real possibility of a complete defeat of the jihadis must also be taken into consideration.

At the same time, this is not an argument for democracies that will be exact copies of the American or European model. The very different conditions in Islamic countries, including a higher tolerance for the integration of religion and government, will lead to the creation of states that reflect the religious, cultural, and historical traditions of that area of the world. Just as the Japanese democratic experience has been far different from that of the West, so too we should not be surprised if Arab or Muslim democracies do not imitate more established models. Yet the fact that Germans and Japanese, Indians and Central Americans have all been able to adapt democracy to local conditions leaves us with hope that the Muslims of the world can find their own path to greater freedom.

Notes

1. Why They Did It

1. Well-known examples of jihadist groups beside al-Qaida include Gama'a al-Islamiya, Islamic Jihad, the original Muslim Brotherhood (and some of its offshoots), Abu Sayyaf, Hizb al-Tahrir, Al-Muhajiroun, Jamaah Islamiyah, the Armed Islamic Group (GIA), the Salafist Group for the [Islamic] Call and Fighting (GSPC), Harakat-ul-Mujahedeen, Jaish-e-Muhammad, Lashkar-e-Jhangvi (implicated in Daniel Pearl's murder), Lashkar-e-Taiba, al-Tawhid, Takfir wal-Hijra, and Salafi Jihad (suspected in the Casablanca bombings).

2. Abu Hamza al-Masri, *What Is Wrong. The Way to Get Shari'a* (Supporters of Shari'a). It should be emphasized again that the following discussion is based on jihadist views, and is not the accepted Islamic or Western view of events.

3. Omer Bakri Mohammad, "The Best Nation," www.obm.clara.net/ Islamic_Topics/Islamic_Concepts/ Best_Nation.htm.

4. Sheikh Abu Al-Waleed Al-Ansari, "The Termination of 'israel': A Qur'anic Fact," *Nida'ul Islam*, no. 20 (Sept–Oct 1997); [Hamas], "The Covenant of the Islamic Resistance Movement (Hamas)," 18 August 1988, http://www.mideastweb.org/hamas.htm; Ahmed Feroze, "The New Form of Colonialism and the Dangers to the Muslim Ummah," *Khilafah Magazine* (December 2000); Abu Dujanah Al-Canadi, "Khilafa: The Dire Need," *Nida'ul Islam*, no. 21 (December–January 1997–98).

5. See, e.g., Hizb-ut-Tahrir, *The Inevitability of the Clash of Civilization* (London: Al-Khilafah, 2002), 36; "The Best Nation," www.obm.clara.net/Islamic_Topics/Islamic_Concepts/Best_Nation.htm; interview with Khomeini on 2 January 1980, "The Religious Scholars Led the Revolt," in Ruhollah Khomeini, *Islam and Revolution* (Berkeley: Mizan Press, 1981), 332.

6. "The Best Nation," www.obm.clara.net/Islamic_Topics/Islamic_Concepts/Best_Nation.htm.

7. A principle called *taqlid.*

8. Talk by Professor Asim Umayra at Najah University, 15 April 2000, "The Destruction of the Khilafah: The Mother of All Crimes," http://www.khilafah.com/home/category.php?DocumentID=233&TagID=24.

9. William E. Shepard, *Sayyid Qutb and Islamic Activism: A Translation and Critical Analysis of Social Justice in Islam* (New York: E. J. Brill, 1996), 277.

10. A constant theme in jihadist writing. See, e.g., speech by 'Issam Amireh (Abu Abdullah) at University of al-Quds, 9 December 2001, "Signs of the Impending Victory," http://www.khilafah.com/home/lographics/category.php?DocumentID=1023&TagID=24.

11. This contention will be dealt with in greater detail in Chapter Five.

12. This is part of their overall strategy to create a new consensus (*ijma'*), a concept that is extremely important within the Sunni community. For

a discussion of *ijma'*, see George Makdis, "Hanbalite Islam," in Merlin L. Swartz, ed., *Studies on Islam* (New York: Oxford University Press, 1981), 253ff.

2. Historical Context

1. See, e.g., Youssef M. Choueiri, *Islamic Fundamentalism* (London: Pinter, 1997); Daniel W. Brown, *Rethinking Tradition in Modern Islamic Thought* (Cambridge: Cambridge University Press, 1996), 29–30; Abdelwahab Meddeb, *The Malady of Islam* (New York: Basic Books, 2003), 44–53, 99–105.

2. For good discussions of Ibn Taymiyya and his thought see: Antony Black, *The History of Islamic Political Thought. From the Prophet to the Present* (Edinburgh: Edinburgh University Press, 2001), 155ff; Emmanuel Sivan, *Radical Islam. Medieval Theology and Modern Politics* (New Haven: Yale University Press, 1985), 94–100.

3. He is, for instance, recognized as a "Shaikh al-Islam"—the highest Sunni title for a cleric, generally granted to only one of the ulama at a time.

4. Shaykh al-Imam Ibn Taymiyya, *Public Duties in Islam. The Institution of the Hisba* (Leicester, U.K.: Islamic Foundation, 1982), 22–23, 117, and throughout.

5. Ibn Taimiyya, *Ibn Taimiyya on Public and Private Law in Islam: Or Public Policy in Islamic Jurisprudence*, trans. Omar A. Farrukh (Beirut, Lebanon: Khayats, 1966), 145. Ibn Taymiyya's entire discussion of jihad makes it one of the major requirements of the faith, another point taken up by the jihadis. Meddeb, *The Malady of Islam*, 44–49. This will be elaborated further in Chapter Seven.

6. *Jahada* (struggle) and *harb* (war), respectively.

7. Taimiyya, *Ibn Taimiyya on Public and Private Law in Islam*, 138.

8. Shaykh al-Islam Ibn Taymiyah, *Al-'Ubudiyyah. Being a True Slave of Allah* (London: Ta-Ha Publishers, 1999), 112–113; the verse is Qur'an 5:54.

9. Ibid., 140–148.

10. For jihadist use of Ibn Taymiyya against those who rule by other than the shari'a, see Johannes J.G. Jansen, *The Neglected Duty. The Creed of Sadat's Assassins and Islamic Resurgence in the Middle East* (New York: MacMillan, 1986), 161–182; "The Stating of the Ijma' on the Kufr of the Rulers Who Rule by What Allah Has Not Revealed," from Abdul-Qadir bin Abdul Aziz, *Al-Jamit Fi Talab-el-Ilm-esh-Sharif*, 2nd ed., vol. 2, 1415 AH, 880–882; Abu Hamza al-Masri, *What Is Wrong. The Way to Get Shari'a* (Supporters of Shari'a); "Ruling by Other Than What Allah Revealed; Tauheed Al-Hakkimyah," *Al-Jihaad*, no. 11, http://www.shareeah.com/Eng/aj/aj11.html; Abu Hamza al-Masri, *Ruling by Man-made Law. Is It Minor or Major Kufr? Explaining the Words of Ibn Abbas* (Supporters of Shari'ah, 1996); 'Usama bin Ladin, "An Open Letter to King Fahd in Response to the Latest Ministerial Changes," http://www.jihadunspun.net/articles/05272002-Open .Letter.To.King.Fahd/.

11. The depth of feeling for Ibn Taymiyya and his views on jihad can be seen by the large number of jihadis and jihadist groups that use his religious rulings (*fatawa*) to justify their resort to open warfare. See, e.g.: Jansen, *The Neglected Duty*, 175–177, 181–182, 207; 'Abdullah 'Azzam, *Defense of the Muslim Lands. The First Obligation After Iman*, n.p., n.d.; Omar Bakri Muhammad, "The Islamic Verdict on: Jihad and the Method to Establish the Khilafah," http://www.geocities.com/ al-khilafah/JIHAD2.htm, 6, 27; Safar bin 'Abdir-Rahmaan al-Hawaali, "A Statement to the Ummah Concerning the Recent Events," http://www.islamicawakening.com/index.htm? (http://www .as-sahwah.com/Articles/bayaan6.phtml); Usama Bin Muhammad Bin Ladin, "Declaration of War Against the Americans Occupying the Land of the Two Holy Places (Expel the Infidels from the Arab Peninsula)," *The Idler* 3, no. 165 (13 September 2001); "A New Bin Laden Speech," 18 July 2003, Middle East Media Research Institute (here-

after MEMRI); Muhammad El-Halaby, "The Role of Sheikh-ul Islam Ibn Taymiyya in Jihad Against the Tatars," *Nida'ul Islam*, no. 17; Sheikh Hammoud Al-Uqlaa Ash-Shuaybi, "Fatwa on Events Following 11 September 2001," http://perso.wanadoo.fr/centralparkattacks/islam.html.

12. There are good discussions of Wahhabism in Hamid Algar, *Wahhabism: A Critical Essay* (Oneonta, NY: Islamic Publications International, 2002); Choueiri, *Islamic Fundamentalism*, 7–11; Brown, *Rethinking Tradition*, 29; Black, *The History of Islamic Political Thought*, 58; Meddeb, *The Malady of Islam*, 53.

13. See Bernard Lewis, *The Emergence of Modern Turkey* (New York: Oxford University Press, 2002), 21–39, for a discussion of the decline of the Ottomans.

14. For the influence of Ibn Taymiyya on Wahhab, see Algar, *Wahhabism*, 8ff.

15. John Obert Voll, *Islam. Continuity and Change in the Modern World*, 2d ed. (Syracuse, NY: Syracuse University Press, 1994), 53–56.

16. *Tawhid al-rububiyya*. Henri Laoust, *Essai sur les doctrines sociales et politiques de Taki-d-Din Ahmad b. Taimiya* (Cairo: Institut Français d'Archéologie Orientale, 1939), 506–540, has a thorough discussion of the connection between Ibn Taymiyya and Wahhab. And see Algar, *Wahhabism*, 31ff, for another good look at Wahhab's interpretation of Islam.

17. *Tawhid al-'ibada*.

18. The name that Wahhab chose for his movement, and which remains the usual term today in Saudi Arabia, was "al-Muwahhidun," meaning those who believed in "tawhid." This was also the name chosen by the ancient purifiers of Islam in North Africa and Spain, whose name Western historians generally transliterate as the "Almohids."

19. Wahhab in fact wrote very little. See, however, 'Usama bin Ladin, "An Open Letter to King Fahd," where he does quote Wahhab.

20. Algar, *Wahhabism*, 3–5.

21. Like Shah Wali Allah, Shah Abdul Aziz, and Sayyid Ahmad Barelewi in India; Uthman dan Fodio in Nigeria; the Grand Ssanusi in Libya; and even the Mahdi of Sudan. John L. Esposito, *Islam and Politics* (Syracuse, NY: Syracuse University Press, 1984), 36–42.

22. See Laoust, *Essai sur les doctrines*, 477–505, and Brown, *Rethinking Tradition*, 29–30.

23. This and the discussion following are taken from Muhammad Rashid Rida, "Renewal, Renewing and Renewers," in Charles Kurzman, ed., *Modernist Islam, 1840–1940. A Sourcebook* (Oxford: Oxford University Press, 2002), 77–85.

24. Quoted in Esposito, *Islam and Politics*, 67.

25. Ibid., 67–68.

26. Sivan, *Radical Islam*, 101–102; see also Laoust, *Essai sur les doctrines*, 557–575, for a thorough discussion of Ibn Taymiyya's influence on Rida.

27. Choueiri, *Islamic Fundamentalism*, 39.

28. Hasan al-Banna, "Our Mission," in *Five Tracts of Hasan Al-Banna. A Selection from the Majmu 'at Rasa'il al-Imam al-Shahid Hasan al-Banna,'* trans. Charles Wendell (Berkeley: University of California Press, 1978), 49–50.

29. This impulse was not, of course, limited to Islamists/jihadis. As Choueiri points out, liberals tended to do the opposite: take Islamic terms and apply them to modern Western concepts. Thus shura (consultation) became "democracy"; *ijma'* (consensus [of the ulama]) became "public opinion"; *maslaha* (public interest) became "utility"; *bay'a* (pledge of loyalty) became "universal suffrage"; ijtihad (reasoning) became "freedom of thought"; *ahl al-hall wa al-'aqd* (those in power, influential people) became "body of elected representatives." Choueiri, *Islamic Fundamentalism*, 22.

30. Ibrahim M. Abu-Rabi', *Intellectual Origins of Islamic Resurgence in the*

Modern Arab World (Albany: State University of New York Press, 1996), 90.

31. Ibid., 80–81.

32. Hasan al-Banna, "Between Yesterday and Today," in *Five Tracts of Hasan Al-Banna*, 30.

33. Ibid., 15. He also advocated a war against poverty, ignorance, disease, and crime. Ibid., 32–33.

34. Hasan al-Banna, "On Jihad," in *Five Tracts of Hasan Al-Banna*, 150; Yousef Al-Qaradawi, *Priorities of the Islamic Movement in the Coming Phase* (Cairo: Dar al Nashr, 1992), 178.

35. Quoted in Fathi Yakan, *To Be a Muslim*, n.p., n.d.

36. Quoted in Meddeb, *The Malady of Islam*, 99.

37. Hasan al-Banna, "To What Do We Summon Mankind?" in *Five Tracts of Hasan Al-Banna*, 71.

38. Ibid., 81.

39. Richard P. Mitchell, *The Society of the Muslim Brothers* (New York: Oxford University Press, 1969).

40. Michael Irving Jensen, "Islamism and Civil Society in the Gaza Strip," in Ahmad S. Moussalli, ed., *Islamic Fundamentalism. Myths & Realities* (Reading: Ithaca, 1998), 215; Shaul Mishal and Avraham Sela, *The Palestinian Hamas. Vision, Violence, and Coexistence* (New York: Columbia University Press, 2000), esp. 156–157; Andrea Nüsse, *Muslim Palestine. The Ideology of Hamas* (Amsterdam: Harwood Academic Publishers, 1998).

41. Since Qutb's thought continues to profoundly affect jihadist groups, we will do no more than outline his philosophy here. A more detailed explication can be found in Chapter Four.

42. Ahmad S. Moussalli, *Radical Islamic Fundamentalism: The Ideological and Political Discourse of Sayyid Qutb* (Beirut: American University of Beirut, 1992), 24–25.

43. For more on Qutb see Choueiri, *Islamic Fundamentalism*, 91–147;

Johannes J. G. Jansen, *The Dual Nature of Islamic Fundamentalism* (London: Hurst, 1997), 49–54; Roxanne L. Euben, *Enemy in the Mirror. Islamic Fundamentalism and the Limits of Modern Rationalism. A Work of Comparative Political Theory* (Princeton, NJ: Princeton University Press, 1999), 49–92; Moussalli, *Radical Islamic Fundamentalism*; Bassam Tibi, *The Challenge of Fundamentalism. Political Islam and the New World Disorder,* updated ed. (Berkeley: University of California Press, 2002), 28–29; Meddeb, *The Malady of Islam,* 101–105.

44. Moussalli, *Radical Islamic Fundamentalism,* 206, 208.
45. Tibi, *The Challenge of Fundamentalism,* 28–29; Seyyed Vali Reza Nasr, *The Vanguard of the Islamic Revolution. The Jama'at-I Islami of Pakistan* (Berkeley: University of California Press, 1994); Sivan, *Radical Islam,* 22–23; Meddeb, *The Malady of Islam,* 101–104.

3. The Qur'an Is Our Constitution

1. See, e.g., Ayatollah Ruhollah Khomeini, *Islamic Government* (New York: Manor Books, 1979), 7. This is also a principle of what is known as "'Ilm al-Usul," or the science of the fundamentals of (Islamic) jurisprudence, generally stated as, "There is no ijtihad [independent reasoning] on clear text."
2. Abu Hamza al-Masri, *What Is Wrong. The Way to Get Shari'a* (Supporters of Shari'a).
3. Jihadis sometimes are categorized as salafi, but this term has several meanings. In the first case, it is a general way of saying "orthodox," and therefore has been used by any Muslims who believe that they are following the correct Islamic path. It has also been applied to a specific movement within Islam (beginning in the late nineteenth century) to return to true Islam, and has therefore come to mean something like "fundamentalist" (of a certain sort). Lately, traditionalist Muslims have been using the term to anathematize the jihadist movement as well as Wahhabis.

4. Abu Hamza al-Masri argues in *What Is Wrong. The Way to Get Shari'a* that only the first three generations of Muslims were righteous and deserve imitation. He is not alone among the jihadis in making this argument, but this has not stopped them from quoting later traditional authorities when these support their actions.

5. al-Tauba 9:29 and al-Baqara 2:193.

6. al-Baqara 2:256 and al-Kafirun 109:6.

7. For a good discussion of abrogation, see Yasin Dutton, *The Origins of Islamic Law. The Qur'an, the Muwatta' and Madinan 'Amal* (Richmond, Surrey: Curzon, 1999), 121–125, and as it specifically applies to jihad in Reuven Firestone, *Jihad. The Origin of Holy War in Islam* (New York: Oxford University Press, 1999), 48–50.

8. Of the six hadith collections, three have been translated in their entirety into English—the two Sahih (Sahih Muslim and Sahih Bukhari), and the Sunan Abu Dawud.

9. This is, of course, the traditional Muslim view of the hadith. Modern scholars contend that there is reason to doubt the validity of many of the hadith.

10. Khaled Abou El Fadl, *The Place of Tolerance in Islam* (Boston: Beacon Press, 2002), 100–101; Sohail H. Hashmi, "A Conservative Legacy," in Abou El Fadl, *The Place of Tolerance in Islam*, 34; Mohammed Arkoun, *Rethinking Islam. Common Questions, Uncommon Answers* (Boulder, CO: Westview Press, 1994), 99.

11. Abou El Fadl, *The Place of Tolerance in Islam*, 23. See also Hashmi, "A Conservative Legacy," 32–33, and Abou El Fadl, *The Place of Tolerance in Islam*, 111.

12. "Attacks from Within: Attempts to Destroy the Islamic 'Aqeedah," 20 July 1998, www.khalifornia.org.

13. ALM Pakistan branch, "The Wishes and Tools of the Kufaar," 24 March 2003, http://homepage.ntlworld.com/mohammed.butt1/sitefiles/short-articles/kafir-unitied-nations-plans-1.htm.

14. "We, the Saudi People, Speak," http://www.boycottusa.org/articles_saudipeople.htm.

15. See Arkoun's interpretation of this in Arkoun, *Rethinking Islam*, 99.

16. Ruhollah Khomeini, "In Commemoration of the First Martyrs of the Revolution [February 19, 1978]," in *Islam and Revolution* (Berkeley: Mizan Press, 1981), 226–227. Many Islamic scholars understood the story of Pharaoh to refer to any despotic ruler. See, e.g., Ibn Taimiyya, *Ibn Taimiyya on Public and Private Law in Islam: Or Public Policy in Islamic Jurisprudence*, trans. Omar A. Farrukh (Beirut, Lebanon: Khayats, 1966), 189; Abul A'la Maududi, *Political Theory of Islam* (Lahore: Islamic Publications, 1976 [1939]), 10–11.

17. See, e.g., Asad Ali, "Muharram and the Fall of Fir'awn," *Khilafah Magazine* (March 2003): 20–22. Lewis notes this phenomenon in Bernard Lewis, *The Crisis of Islam. Holy War and Unholy Terror* (New York: Modern Library, 2003), xxiii–xxiv.

18. See "Bin Laadin Speaks on Hijrah; And The Islamic Emirate of Afghanistan," *Al-Jihaad*, no. 4.

19. "Qiyam ul Lail: The Battle of Badr Compared to the Battle for Chechnya," www.shu.ac.uk.

20. Moulana Mohammed Masood Azhar, *The Virtues of Jihad* (Ahle Sunnah Wal Jama'at, 1996), 111–120.

21. Sheikh Hammoud Al-Uqlaa Ash-Shuaybi, "Fatwa on Events Following 11 September 2001," http://perso.wanadoo.fr/centralparkattacks/islam.html.

22. Azhar, *The Virtues of Jihad*, 112.

23. Sayyid Qutb, "Our Struggle with the Jews" ("Ma'rakatuna Ma'a al-Yahud"), in Ronald L. Nettler, *Past Trials and Present Tribulations. A Muslim Fundamentalist's View of the Jews* (Oxford: Pergamon, 1987); Sheikh Muhammad Al-'Uthaymeen, "The Jews and Their Treachery," http://www.islamicawakening.com/viewarticle.php?articleID=940; Sheikh Abu Al-Waleed Al-Ansari, "The Termina-

tion of 'israel': A Qur'anic Fact," *Nida'ul Islam*, no. 20 (Sept.–Oct. 1997).

24. Sayyid Qutb, *In the Shade of the Qur'an (Fi Zilal al-Qur'an)*, vol. 1 (Markfield, Leicester: The Islamic Foundation, 1999), 17. Qutb had much more to say about the perfidy of the Jews as revealed in the sacred texts in Qutb, "Our Struggle with the Jews," 72–89.

25. Khomeini, *Islamic Government*, 31; [Hamas], "The Covenant of the Islamic Resistance Movement (Hamas)," 18 August 1988, http://www.mideastweb.org/hamas.htm.

26. [Hizb ut-Tahrir], *The American Campaign to Suppress Islam* (London: Al-Khilafah Publications, 1996), 15.

27. See the draft constitution for an Islamic state in [Hizb-ut-Tahrir], *The System of Islam* (London: Al-Khilafah Publications, 2002); also Asif Khan, "Exposition of Capitalism—The Corrupted Creed, [Part 3] Democracy," http://www.mindspring.eu.com/capitalismp3.htm; Zafar Bangash, "The Concepts of Leader and Leadership in Islam," in *ICIT Papers on Muslim Political Thought*, The Institute of Contemporary Islamic Thought, n.d.; Abu Mustafa Al Bansilwani, "Encounter with Islam: Presence of the Prophet Is Not Necessary to Reestablish the Islamic State," in Iyad Hilal, ed., *Selections from the Seerah of Muhammad* (London: Khilafah Publications, n.d.), 73; Iyad Hilal, "Usul al-Fiqh: The Authority of Sunnah," in ibid., 25–31.

28. Everywhere, but see especially Jamaal al-ddin Zarabozo, "The Importance of Jihad in the Life of a Muslim," *Al-Bashir Magazine*, n.d.; Azhar, *The Virtues of Jihad*; "Lessons from the Battle of the Trench," *As-Sahwa* 3, no. 1 (October 2001): 4–6.

29. A fact pointed out by many scholars. See, e.g., Nazih N. Ayubi, *Political Islam. Religion and Politics in the Arab World* (London; Routledge, 1991), 3; Bassam Tibi, *The Challenge of Fundamentalism. Political Islam and the New World Disorder*, updated ed. (Berkeley: University of California Press, 2002), 68, 99; Lewis, *The Crisis of Islam*, 138.

30. For good discussions of the traditional asbab al-nuzul see Dutton, *The Origins of Islamic Law*, 125–130, and Firestone, *Jihad*, 48–50.

4. Our 'Aqida

1. Armando Salvatore, *Islam and the Political Discourse of Modernity* (Reading, Berkshire: Garnet Publishing, 1997), 203.

2. William E. Shepard, *Sayyid Qutb and Islamic Activism: A Translation and Critical Analysis of Social Justice in Islam* (New York: E. J. Brill, 1996), 24.

3. Sayyid Qutb, *Islam. The Religion of the Future* (Delhi: Markazi Maktaba Islam, 1990), 50, 67.

4. Abul A'la Maududi, *Jihad in Islam* [*Jihad fi Sabil Allah*] (Lagos: Ibrash Islamic Publications Centre, 1939), 15; Shepard, *Sayyid Qutb and Islamic Activism*, 108–110; Hizb-ut-Tahrir, "The Campaign to Subvert Islam as an Ideology and a System," 16 October 2001, http://www.1924.org/leaflets/index.php?id=30_0_10_0_C; [Hizb-ut-Tahrir], *The System of Islam*, (London: Al-Khilafah Publications, 2002); "Editorial Statement," *Khilafah Magazine*; [Taliban], *Jihad: The Foreign Policy of the Islamic State*, http://ayeko.s5.com/Taliban/Jihad.html. See also Bassam Tibi, *The Challenge of Fundamentalism. Political Islam and the New World Disorder*, updated ed. (Berkeley: University of California Press, 2002), 138–139; Salvatore, *Islam and the Political Discourse of Modernity*, 192.

5. Shepard, *Sayyid Qutb and Islamic Activism*, 24, 29–33; Fathi Yakan, *To Be a Muslim*, n.p., n.d.; Asif Khan, "The Battle Over the Masjid," *Khilafah Magazine*, May 2003: 19–21; [Hizb-ut-Tahrir], *The System of Islam*; "Attacks from Within: Attempts to Destroy the Islamic 'Aqeedah," 20 July 1998: www.khalifornia.org.

6. Shepard, *Sayyid Qutb and Islamic Activism*, 33.

7. Abul A'la Maududi, *Political Theory of Islam* (Lahore: Islamic Publications, 1976 [1939]), 8.

8. Maududi, *Political Theory of Islam*, 10, 15, 16 (emphasis his).

9. A'la Maududi, *Jihad in Islam*, 12–13.

10. Maududi, *Political Theory of Islam*, 20; see also Abul A'la Maududi, *The Moral Foundations of the Islamic Movement* (Lahore: Islamic Publications, 1976), 36; Abul 'Ala Maudoodi, *The Process of Islamic Revolution*, 2d ed. (Lahore: Maktaba Jama'at-e-Islami Pakistan, 1955), 15.

11. Maududi, *Political Theory of Islam*, 22; Sayyid Abul A'la Maududi, *Short History of the Revivalist Movement in Islam* [*Tajdid-o-Ihya-i-Din*, 1940] (Lahore: Islamic Publications, 1963), 17–22; Maududi, *Jihad in Islam*, 10.

12. Sayyid Qutb, *Milestones* (Delhi: Markazi Maktaba Islami, 1991), 102.

13. Shepard, *Sayyid Qutb and Islamic Activism*, 43; Qutb, *Milestones*, 113.

14. Qutb, *Milestones*, 40–41.

15. Sayyid Qutb, *In the Shade of the Qur'an* [*Fi Zilal al-Qur'an*], vol. 6 (Markfield, Leicester: The Islamic Foundation, 2002), 163; Sayyid Qutb, *Milestones*, 61.

16. Qutb, *Milestones*, 83–84 (emphasis mine).

17. Qutb, *Milestones*, 108.

18. See Kepel's discussion of this point in Gilles Kepel, *Muslim Extremism in Egypt. The Prophet and Pharaoh* (Berkeley: University of California Press, [1984] 2003), 24–25.

19. Shepard, *Sayyid Qutb and Islamic Activism*, 277–279; Qutb, *Milestones*, 142–145, 152–153.

20. Qutb, *Milestones*, 85.

21. Qutb, *Milestones*, 177.

22. Qutb, *Milestones*, 14–15.

23. Sayyid Qutb, *In the Shade of the Qur'an* [*Fi Zilal al-Qur'an*], vol. 5 (Markfield, Leicester: The Islamic Foundation, 2002), 38–39; Qutb, *Milestones*, 148–153.

24. This is also a general Islamic term for Islam, but jihadis emphasize the absolute and comprehensive truth of Islam: outside Islam there is nothing but lies and vanity. See especially Qutb, *Milestones*, 244, 269; Shepard, *Sayyid Qutb and Islamic Activism*, 108; Sheikh Ali 'Abdur Rah-

maan Hudhayfi, "Historic Khutbah," http://www.jamiat.org.za/
isinfo/huzaifi.html; "Attacks from Within: Attempts to Destroy the
Islamic 'Aqeedah"; Hizb-ut-Tahrir, *The Inevitability of the Clash of
Civilization* (London: Al-Khilafah, 2002), 17, 50–52; Hizb-ut-Tahrir,
"The Campaign to Subvert Islam as an Ideology and a System"; "Are
They the People of the Book?; Question and Answers," *Al-Jihaad*, no.
2, http://www.shareeah.com/Eng/aj/aj2.html.

25. And also within the Iranian revolution. Khomeini, in an interview
from 1980, said that "the sole determining principle in a government
based on tawhid is divine law, law that is the expression of divine will,
not the product of the human mind." Interview with Khomeini on 2
January 1980, "The Religious Scholars Led the Revolt," in Ruhollah
Khomeini, *Islam and Revolution* (Berkeley: Mizan Press, 1981), 330.

26. Shaikh 'Abd ul-Qadir bin 'Abd ul-Aziz, "The Stating of the Ijma
on the Kufr of the Rulers Who Rule by What Allah Has Not Revealed," *Al-Jami' Fi Talab-al-'Ilm- al-Sharif*, 2d ed., vol. 2 (n.p.,
1994), 880–882.

27. http://www.islamic-truth.fsnet.co.uk.

28. Abu Dujanah Al-Canadi, "Khilafa: The Dire Need," *Nida'ul Islam*, no.
21 (December 1997–January 1998).

29. See, e.g., Hizb-ut-Tahrir, *The System of Islam*. Almost every article in
the Hizb-ut-Tahrir magazine *Khilafah* deals with the need to legislate
with God's laws alone. See, e.g., Sabure Malik, "The Astute Comprehension of International Law," *Khilafah Magazine* 16, no. 1 (January
2003): 11; Abdul-Hamid Jassat and Dilpazier Aslam, "Differentiating
Between Tradition and Islam," *Khilafah Magazine* (May 2003): 30;
"The Matrix: Hollywood 'Reloads' Disbelief in Allah," *Khilafah Magazine* (July 2003): 17. Other articles argue that Islam no longer exists
anywhere, and that all Islamic lands are unbelieving. See [Hizb ut-
Tahrir], *The Methodology of Hizb ut-Tahrir for Change* (London: Al-
Khilafah Publications, 1999), 10–11, 24, 30–31.

30. Fathi Yakan, *To Be a Muslim*, n.p., n.d. By materialism, jihadis mean the idea that the material universe is all that exists. Their critique of materialism is thus aimed primarily at Marxists and other secularists who deny the existence of God and the afterlife.

31. Kalim Siddiqui, "Processes of Error, Deviation, Correction and Convergence in Muslim Political Thought," *ICIT Papers on Muslim Political Thought* (The Institute of Contemporary Islamic Thought); Kalim Siddiqui, "Political Dimensions of the Seerah," *ICIT Papers on the Seerah* (The Institute of Contemporary Islamic Thought); Zafar Bangash, "The Concepts of Leader and Leadership in Islam," *ICIT Papers on Muslim Political Thought* (The Institute of Contemporary Islamic Thought). The ICIT, although generally seen as an Islamist rather than jihadist institution, publicly supports armed struggle against the unbelievers. The concept of jahiliyya as argued by Qutb has influenced the thought of many jihadis. See, e.g., Shamim A. Siddiqi, *The Revival of the Muslim Ummah* (New York: Forum for Islamic Work, 1996), 64, 71–72.

32. See his interpolation in the verse "And fight them until there is no more Fitnah (Shirk, oppression or absence of Shari'a) and the religion in totality is for Allah." Abu Hamza al-Masri, *The Need for Shari'a* (Supporters of Shari'ah, n.d.).

33. Abu Hamza al-Masri, *Ruling by Man-made Law. Is It Minor or Major Kufr? Explaining the Words of Ibn Abbas* (Supporters of Shari'ah, 1996).

34. 'Usama bin Ladin, "An Open Letter to King Fahd in Response to the Latest Ministerial Changes," http://www.jihadunspun.net/articles/05272002-Open.Letter.To.King.Fahd/.

35. Specific acts or declarations that make a Muslim into an apostate or heretic and therefore liable to be killed.

36. 'Usama Bin Muhammad Bin Ladin, "Declaration of War Against the Americans Occupying the Land of the Two Holy Places (Expel the

Infidels from the Arab Peninsula)," *The Idler* 3, no. 165 (13 September 2001).

37. "Bin Laadin Speaks on Hijrah; And the Islamic Emirate of Afghanistan," *Al-Jihaad*, no. 4.

38. [Hizb ut-Tahrir], *The American Campaign to Suppress Islam* (London: Al-Khilafah, 1996), 13; [Hizb ut-Tahrir], *Dangerous Concepts to Attack Islam and Consolidate the Western Culture* (London: Al-Khilafah, 1997), 28.

39. Shepard, *Sayyid Qutb and Islamic Activism*, 2–3; OBM Network ['Umar Bakri Muhammad], "Islam vs. Democracy," n.d.; Fathi Yakan, "Distinguishing the Movement from Specialized Organizations," *To Be a Muslim*, n.p., n.d.

40. See [Hamas], "The Covenant of the Islamic Resistance Movement (Hamas)," 18 August 1988, http://www.mideastweb.org/hamas.htm.

41. "Re-establishing the Khilafah State Is the Only Way to Free Ourselves from the Oppression of the Western Colonial Powers," 10 March 10 2003, http://www.1924.org/leaflets/index.php?id= 151_0_10_0_M#; see also Asif Khan, "The Battle Over the Masjid," *Khilafah Magazine* (May 2003): 20.

42. [Hizb ut-Tahrir], *The System of Islam*.

43. Qutb, *Islam. The Religion of the Future*, 43.

44. Maududi, *Political Theory of Islam*, 22.

45. Shepard, *Sayyid Qutb and Islamic Activism*, 108–112.

46. [Hizb ut-Tahrir], *How the Khilafah Was Destroyed*, n.p., n.d., 29–31.

47. Abdul-Hamid Jassat, "It Is Haram to Support Kufr Political Parties," *Khilafah Magazine* (June 2001).

48. Sheikh Omar Bakri Muhammad, "Sharing Power with Kufr Regimes or Voting for Man-Made Law Is Prohibited (Haram)," www.obm.clara .net/islamicissues/voting.html. The sentiment is echoed by another jihadist-in-exile, Abu Hamza al-Masri, in "Questions & Answers; Fiqh, Aqeedah, Tafsir, Fatwa, Jihaad, Minhaj," *Al-Jihaad*, no. 1. In this

article Abu Hamza cites the supporting opinion of a recognized scholar of Islamic law, Muhammad Amin al-Shanqiti, a professor at the Islamic University of Madinah.

49. Literally "consultation."

50. Zafar Bangash, "The Concepts of Leader and Leadership in Islam," *ICIT Papers on Muslim Political Thought* (The Institute of Contemporary Islamic Thought).

51. [Hizb ut-Tahrir], *The System of Islam*. 'Umar Bakri Muhammad argues that in any case there can be no international law without an international state to enforce those laws. OBM Network, "Politics—The International Law," n.d.

52. Jilani Gulam, "The Fallacy of International Law," *Khilafah Magazine* (April 2003): 18–19.

53. Sabure Malik, "The Astute Comprehension of International Law," *Khilafah Magazine* 16, no. 1 (January 2003): 10.

54. Asif Khan, "Exposition of Capitalism—The Corrupted Creed [Part 2]," http://www.mindspring.eu.com/capitalismp2.htm; Sabure Malik, "The UN a Tool of Exploitation by the Colonialists," *Khilafah Magazine* (March 2003): 14–16; [Hizb ut-Tahrir], *The Inevitability of the Clash of Civilization* (London: Al-Khilafah, 2002), 46; Anjem Choudary, "Divine Human Rights or Man-Made Human Rights," [Al-Muhajiroun, 1998(?)]; "Afghanistan Is Not an Islamic State," http://www.islamic-state.org/afghanistan/.

55. Sayyid Qutb, *In the Shade of the Qur'an [Fi Zilal al-Qur'an]*, vol. 1 (Markfield, Leicester: The Islamic Foundation, 1999), 355, 357.

56. Sayyid Qutb, *In the Shade of the Qur'an [Fi Zilal al-Qur'an]*, vol. 2 (Markfield, Leicester: The Islamic Foundation, 2000), 212.

57. 'Usama bin Ladin, "An Open Letter to King Fahd."

58. 'Usama Bin Muhammad Bin Ladin, "Declaration of War Against the Americans Occupying the Land of the Two Holy Places (Expel the Infidels from the Arab Peninsula)," *The Idler* 3, no. 165 (13 September

2001). Other jihadis also mention the Saʿudi permitting of usury as a reason to attack that government. See "Treachery from the Peninsula; Government Scholars Destroying Islam," *Al-Jihaad*, no. 4.

59. "Statement by al-Qaida," *The Observer*, 24 November 2002. For other jihadist statements tying Jewish people to usury see Qutb, *Milestones*, 207; "Palestine Issue Looms Overhead; Jewish Extremists Continue Their Reign of Terror," *Al-Jihaad*, no. 9, http://www.shareeah.com/Eng/aj/aj9.html.

60. Safar bin ʿAbdir-Rahmaan al-Hawaali, "A Statement to the Ummah Concerning the Recent Events," http://www.islamicawakening.com/index.htm? (http://www.as-sahwah.com/Articles/bayaan6.phtml).

61. Shepard, *Sayyid Qutb and Islamic Activism*, 134.

62. [Hizb ut-Tahrir], "A Draft Constitution," *The System of Islam*.

63. See, e.g., Babar Qureshi, "Iraq—The Cradle of Civilisation," *Khilafah Magazine* (April 2003): 20–22; Dawud, "American Justice," *Khilafah Magazine* (June 2003): 25–26; "The despicable submission of the rulers before the open American aggression," http://www.islamic-state.org/leaflets/030129_DespicableSubmissionOfRulersBeforeAmerican Aggression.php.

64. "Statement by al-Qaida."

65. It is not too much to claim that this is the theme of his seminal work, *Milestones*. See, e.g., Qutb, *Milestones*, 63, 102–111, 113, 117, 125, 128–139, 177–179. One could speculate that his insistence on this point might have been provoked by criticisms of Islam that he encountered while in the United States in the late forties and early fifties.

66. Maududi, *Political Theory of Islam*, 27–30.

67. [Hizb ut-Tahrir], *The American Campaign to Suppress Islam*, 23, 31ff.

68. Anjem Choudary, "Divine Human Rights or Man-Made Human Rights," [Al-Muhajiroun, 1998(?)].

69. OBM Network, "Islam vs. Democracy," n.d.

70. "Qiyam ul Lail: The Battle of Badr Compared to the Battle for Chechnya." www.shu.ac.uk.

71. Qutb, *In the Shade of the Qur'an*, vol. 1, 85, 117, 126; Sayyid Qutb, *In the Shade of the Qur'an [Fi Zilal al-Qur'an]*, vol. 3 (Markfield, Leicester: The Islamic Foundation, 2001), 372–373; Sayyid Qutb, *In the Shade of the Qur'an [Fi Zilal al-Qur'an]*, vol. 4 (Markfield, Leicester: The Islamic Foundation, 2001), 146–147, 184; Qutb, *In the Shade of the Qur'an*, vol. 6, 239.

72. [Hizb ut-Tahrir], "The Campaign to Subvert Islam as an Ideology and a System," 16 October 2001, http://www.1924.org/leaflets/index.php?id=30_0_10_0_C; "Attacks from Within: Attempts to Destroy the Islamic 'Aqeedah," 20 July 1998, www.khalifornia.org.

73. See, e.g., Qutb, *In the Shade of the Qur'an*, vol. 1, 56–58, 91, 114, 160; Qutb, *In the Shade of the Qur'an*, vol. 2, 52–53, 118–121; Qutb, *In the Shade of the Qur'an*, vol. 3, 172–173, 182–183; Qutb, *In the Shade of the Qur'an*, vol. 4, 144, 150–151, 166–171, 205, 218–221, 227–230; Sayyid Qutb, *In the Shade of the Qur'an (Fi Zilal al-Qur'an)*, vol. 5 (Markfield, Leicester: The Islamic Foundation, 2002), 37–40, 133–135, 311–312; Qutb, *In the Shade of the Qur'an*, vol. 6, 25, 232–233, 237–238, 250.

74. See, e.g., Qutb, *In the Shade of the Qur'an*, vol. 4, 221–227.

75. "Are They the People of the Book?; Question and Answers," *Al-Jihaad*, no. 2, http://www.shareeah.com/Eng/aj/aj2.html.

76. "Integration—Al-Indimaaj," *As-Sahwa* (November 2001): 10.

77. The link between this desire to destroy liberalism and September 11 will be explored in greater depth in the next chapter.

5. *The Clash of Civilizations, Part I*

1. Although 'Usama bin Ladin and other jihadis have not hesitated to agree that there is indeed a "clash of civilizations." See Tayseer Allouni with Usamah bin Laden, "The Unreleased Interview, 21 October

2001," from Markaz Derasat (translated by Muawiya ibn Abi Sufyan), http://www.islamicawakening.org/print.php?articleID=977 (http://www.as-sahwah.com); [Hizb-ut-Tahrir], *The Inevitability of the Clash of Civilization* (London: Al-Khilafah, 2002).

2. See, e.g., Shaykh Abu Muhammad al-Maqdisi, *This Is Our Aqidah!* n.p., n.d., 10; "Re-establishing the Khilafah State Is the Only Way to Free Ourselves from the Oppression of the Western Colonial Powers," 10 March 2003, http://www.1924.org/leaflets/index.php?id= 151_0_10_0_M#; "Farewell Message from Azzam Publications," 20 November 2001, www.azzam.com; Sayyid Qutb, *In the Shade of the Qur'an [Fi Zilal al-Qur'an]*, vol. 1 (Markfield, Leicester: The Islamic Foundation, 1999), 55; Sayyid Qutb, *In the Shade of the Qur'an [Fi Zilal al-Qur'an]*, vol. 6 (Markfield, Leicester: The Islamic Foundation, 2002), 123, 127, 136, 147, 178, 181, 184, 253; Sayyid Qutb, *Milestones* (Delhi: Markazi Maktaba Islami, 1991), 116–117. Qutb dates the struggle between "truth (*haqq*) and falsehood (batil), faith (*iman*) and rejection (kufr)," to the first encounter between Moses and Pharaoh, a significant point since he equates "falsehood" with "tyranny" (*taghut*). Qutb, *In the Shade of the Qur'an*, vol. 6, 178. Hatana shows Islamic Jihad's conviction that the conflict in Israel and Palestine are part of this eternal battle in Meir Hatana, *Islam and Salvation in Palestine. The Islamic Jihad Movement* (Tel Aviv: Tel Aviv University, 2001), 48.

3. "Attacks from Within: Attempts to Destroy the Islamic 'Aqeedah," 20 July 1998, www.khalifornia.org; [Hizb ut-Tahrir], *Dangerous Concepts to Attack Islam and Consolidate the Western Culture* (London: Al-Khilafah, 1997). Qutb argued that "it is in the nature of things that the very existence of the truth is a source of trouble to falsehood, making a battle between the two inevitable. This is how God has ordained things." Qutb, *In the Shade of the Qur'an*, vol. 6, 147.

4. Moulana Mohammed Masood Azhar, *The Virtues of Jihad [Ahle Sunnah Wal Jama'at]*, n.p., n.d., 112.

5. OBM Network, "Treaties in Islam," n.d.

6. Qutb, *In the Shade of the Qur'an*, vol. 1, 56; Sayyid Qutb, *In the Shade of the Qur'an [Fi Zilal al-Qur'an]*, vol. 2 (Markfield, Leicester: The Islamic Foundation, 2000), 147; Sayyid Qutb, *In the Shade of the Qur'an [Fi Zilal al-Qur'an]*, vol. 3 (Markfield, Leicester: The Islamic Foundation, 2001), 172–173, 182; Sayyid Qutb, *In the Shade of the Qur'an [Fi Zilal al-Qur'an]*, vol. 4 (Markfield, Leicester: The Islamic Foundation, 2001), 56–57, 218, 220; Qutb, *In the Shade of the Qur'an*, vol. 6, 237–238; Sayyid Qutb, *In the Shade of the Qur'an [Fi Zilal al-Qur'an]*, vol. 8 (Markfield, Leicester: The Islamic Foundation, 2003), 113–115.

7. Sayyid Qutb, "Our Struggle with the Jews" ["Ma'rakatuna Ma'a al-Yahud"], in Ronald L. Nettler, *Past Trials and Present Tribulations. A Muslim Fundamentalist's View of the Jews* (Oxford: Pergamon, 1987), 72–89.

8. Azhar, *The Virtues of Jihad*, 32, 112–120; Sheikh Abu Al-Waleed Al-Ansari, "The Termination of 'israel': A Qur'anic Fact," *Nida'ul Islam*, no. 20 (Sept.–Oct. 1997); Sheikh Ali 'Abdur Rahmaan Hudhayfi, "Historic Khutbah," http://www.jamiat.org.za/isinfo/huzaifi.html; [Hizb-ut-Tahrir], "The Muslim Ummah Will Never Submit to the Jews," 3 November 1999, http://www.hizb-ut-tahrir.org/english/leaflets/palestine31199.htm. This is a view shared by even less radical Muslim scholars. See Kamal Ahmad Own [vice-principal of Tanta Institute], "The Jews Are the Enemies of Human Life as Is Evident from Their Holy Book," Academy of Islamic Research, Al Azhar, *The Fourth Conference of the Academy of Islamic Research* (Cairo: General Organization of Government Printing Offices, 1968), 361–392; Moh. Taha Yahia, "The Attitude of the Jews Towards Islam and Muslims in the Early Days of Islam," in ibid., 393–397; Abdel Aziz Kamil, "Jewish Role in Aggression on the Islamic Base in Medina," in ibid., 399–414; Sheikh Abd Allah Al Meshad, "Jews' Attitude Towards Islam and Muslims in the First Islamic Era," in ibid., 415–465; Muhammad Azzah Darwaza, "The Atti-

tude of the Jews Toward Islam, Muslims and the Prophet of Islam—
P.B.U.H. at the Time of His Honourable Prophethood," in ibid.,
467–496.

9. PBS *Frontline*, "Who Is Osama Bin Laden?" May 1998,
http://www.jihadunspun.com/BinLadensNetwork/interviews/
pbsfrontline05–1998.cfm.

10. See, e.g., "Islamic Jihad in Indonesia; Tears and Fears for the Unholy
Coming," *Al-Jihaad*, no. 10.

11. "Be Afraid, Be Very Afraid; Sincere Advice o the Believers," *Al-Jihaad*,
no. 3; Qutb, "Our Struggle with the Jews," 83.

12. His usual term for Jews and Christians.

13. A proposition also agreed to by Sheikh Hudhayfi. See Hudhayfi, "Historic Khutbah."

14. Qutb, *In the Shade of the Qur'an*, vol. 1, 90–91; Qutb, *In the Shade of the
Qur'an*, vol. 2, 123. Other jihadis agree. See, e.g., Al-Ansari, "The Termination of 'israel.'"

15. The general jihadist interpretation of the word *taghut*, a Qur'anic term
that means "idolatry" or "false gods."

16. [Hizb ut-Tahrir], *How the Khilafah Was Destroyed*, n.p., n.d.

17. Hani Jamal Eldin, "March 3rd 1924," *Khilafah Magazine* (March
2003): 8–10.

18. An important concept that is discussed in detail below.

19. [Hamas], "The Covenant of the Islamic Resistance Movement (Hamas),"
article 35, 18 August 1988, http://www.mideastweb.org/hamas.htm.

20. [Hizb ut-Tahrir], *How the Khilafah Was Destroyed*.

21. Even some Islamists agree that this was the reason for Israel's establishment. Abdullah Kannoun, "Muslims and the Problem of Palestine," *The Fourth Conference of the Academy of Islamic Research*, n.p., 254.

22. And certainly have never been forgotten by the jihadis. See Sheikh
Safar Al-Hawali, "Open Letter to President Bush," 15 October 2001,

http://www.muslimuzbekistan.com/eng/ennews/2001/10/
ennews20102001.html.

23. William E. Shepard, *Sayyid Qutb and Islamic Activism: A Translation and Critical Analysis of Social Justice in Islam* (New York: E. J. Brill, 1996), 282–283.

24. Ibid., 287–288.

25. Ibid., 286. See, too, Qutb, *In the Shade of the Qur'an*, vol. 6, 166.

26. Sayyid Qutb, *Islam. The Religion of the Future* (Delhi: Markazi Maktaba Islam, 1990), 83.

27. Shepard, *Sayyid Qutb and Islamic Activism*, 282–283.

28. Qutb, *In the Shade of the Qur'an*, vol. 1, 114. Khomeini agrees with this view of imperialism (as a Western movement primarily directed against Islam). See Ayatollah Ruhollah Khomeini, *Islamic Government* (New York: Manor Books, 1979), 6, 10, 12ff. The idea that one of the major purposes of imperialism was to destroy Islam—and that this continues today—is not confined to jihadis. See Abid Ullah Jan, "The Limits of Tolerance," in Khaled Abou El Fadl, *The Place of Tolerance in Islam* (Boston: Beacon Press, 2002), 44.

29. Qutb, *Milestones*, 303.

30. Asif Khan, "Exposition of Capitalism—The Corrupted Creed [Part 2]," http://www.mindspring.eu.com/capitalismp2.htm.

31. [Hamas], "The Covenant of the Islamic Resistance Movement (Hamas)."

32. Qutb, *Milestones*, 125, 137–138; [Hizb ut-Tahrir], *How the Khilafah Was Destroyed*; "21st Century Crusade Against Islam," *As-Sahwa* 3, no. 1 (October 2001): 3.

33. Richard P. Mitchell, *The Society of the Muslim Brothers* (New York: Oxford University Press, 1969), 229; Hasan al-Banna, "Between Yesterday and Today," *Five Tracts of Hasan Al-Banna. A Selection from the Majmu 'at Rasa'il al-Imam al-Shahid Hasan al-Banna,'* trans. Charles

Wendell (Berkeley: University of California Press, 1978), 30; Qutb, *Milestones*, 124–125.

34. Qutb, *In the Shade of the Qur'an*, vol. 2, 120.

35. Sayyid Qutb, *In the Shade of the Qur'an [Fi Zilal al-Qur'an]*, vol. 5 (Markfield, Leicester: The Islamic Foundation, 2002), 87–89.

36. Qutb, *In the Shade of the Qur'an*, vol. 1, 114.

37. Qutb, *In the Shade of the Qur'an*, vol. 2, 10.

38. "Attacks from Within: Attempts to destroy the Islamic 'Aqeedah."

39. Asim Umayra, "The Destruction of the Khilafah: The Mother Of All Crimes," talk given at Najah University, 15 April 2000, http://www.khilafah.com/home/category.php?DocumentID= 233&TagID=24.

40. Qutb, *In the Shade of the Qur'an*, vol. 5, 134; Sahid-Ivan Salam, "Hajj. The Political Significance," *Khilafah Magazine* 16, no. 2 (February 2003): 8–11.

41. Shamim A. Siddiqi, *The Revival of the Muslim Ummah* (New York: Forum for Islamic Work, 1996); Qutb, *Islam. The Religion of the Future*, 6–7.

42. [Hizb ut-Tahrir], "The Khilafah Was Destroyed in Turkey 79 Years Ago; So Let the Righteous Khilafah Be Declared Again in Turkey," 22 February 2003, http://www.hizb-ut-tahrir.org/english/leaflets/ february2203.htm; "Turkey Joins the War Against Islam," *As-Sahwa* (November 2001): 12; Umayra, "The Destruction of the Khilafah: The Mother of All Crimes."

43. See, e.g., Hani Jamal Eldin, "March 3rd 1924."

44. "21st Century Crusade Against Islam," 3; [Hizb ut-Tahrir], "The Khilafah Was Destroyed in Turkey 79 Years Ago;" Umayra, "The Destruction of the Khilafah." Khomeini was one of the first Islamic thinkers to articulate this position. See Khomeini, *Islamic Government*, 26.

45. Kalim Siddiqui, "Processes of Error, Deviation, Correction and Con-

vergence in Muslim Political Thought," *ICIT Papers on Muslim Political Thought* (The Institute of Contemporary Islamic Thought, 1989).

46. [Hizb ut-Tahrir], "The Campaign to Subvert Islam as an Ideology and a System."

47. Qutb, *In the Shade of the Qur'an*, vol. 5, 39; [Hizb ut-Tahrir], "The Muslim Ummah Will Never Submit to the Jews," 3 November 1999, http://www.hizb-ut-tahrir.org/english/leaflets/palestine31199.htm; "The Despicable Submission of the Rulers Before the Open American Aggression," http://www.islamic-state.org/leaflets/030129_DespicableSubmissionOf RulersBeforeAmericanAggression.php; [Hizb ut-Tahrir], *The American Campaign to Suppress Islam* (London: Al-Khilafah Publications, 1996), 9, 12; Mufti Khubiab Sahib, *Zaad e Mujahid* (*Essential Provision of the Mujahid*), n.p., n.d., 45–46; [Hizb ut-Tahrir], "The Peace (Surrender) Process in the Middle East," 12 June 1998, http://www.hizb-ut-tahrir.org/english/leaflets/surrender.htm.

48. Siddiqi, *The Revival of the Muslim Ummah*, 8–9; "Attacks from Within;" Ahmed Feroze, "The New Form of Colonialism and the Dangers to the Muslim Ummah," *Khilafah Magazine* (December 2000); Ahmer Sajid, "The Treachery of the Rulers of Muslims in the 4th Crusade," *Khilafah Magazine* (April 2003): 12–13.

49. [No Author], *The Pirate State of Saudi Arabia: From Past to Present Day* (MNA Publications), n.d.; Dawud, "American Justice," *Khilafah Magazine* (June 2003): 25–26; "Holy Lands Have a British Consulate; Saudi Rulers Must Leave or Die!" *Al-Jihaad*, no. 2; Abu Hamza al-Masri, *The Need for Shari'a* (Supporters of Shari'ah).

50. [Hizb ut-Tahrir], *How the Khilafah Was Destroyed*.

51. His first discussion of all these issues was in Usama bin Ladin, "An Open Letter to King Fahd."

52. "Mujahid Usamah Bin Ladin Talks Exclusively to 'Nida'ul Islam' About the New Powder Keg in The Middle East," *Nida'ul Islam*, no. 15 (October/November 1996); "ABC Interview with Osama

bin Laden," January 1998, http://www.jihadunspun.net/
BinLadensNetwork/interviews/abc01-1998.cfm.

53. "Statement by al-Qaida," *The Observer,* 24 November 2002.

54. See Shabir Ahmed, "France Ready to Oppose American and British Post-War Plans for Iraq," *Khilafah Magazine* (April 2003): 6; "A Letter from Members of Hizb ut-Tahrir Britain to Yusuf al-Qaradhawi on His Visit," *Khilafah Magazine* 16, no. 2 (February 2003): 16–17.

55. [Hizb ut-Tahrir], *The American Campaign to Suppress Islam,* 7–8; "Holy Lands Have a British Consulate; Saudi Rulers Must Leave or Die!" *Al-Jihaad,* no. 2, http://www.shareeah.com/Eng/aj/aj2.html; OBM, "The Humiliation of Muslims by America: U.S. Expansionist," *Islamic Spotlight,* no. 26, n.p., n.d.; Abdul Salam Zaeef, "America's Military Campaign in the Region," *The Frontier Post,* Peshawar, http://www.islamicawakening.com/index.htm? (http://www.as-sahwah.com/Articles/).

56. Shamin A. Siddiqi, *Methodology of Dawah il Allah in American Perspective* (New York: Forum For Islamic Work, 1989), 68. See also "Holy Lands Have a British Consulate; Saudi Rulers Must Leave or Die!" *Al-Jihaad,* no. 2, http://www.shareeah.com/Eng/aj/aj2.html.

57. "The West and the Zionists–Who Controls Who?" Translated from *Al-Waie,* 24 November 2000, http://www.khilafah.com/home/category.php?DocumentID=654&TagID=24.

58. Azzam Publications, "Translation of Interview with Dr. Ayman al Zawaahri," September 2002, http://www.mediareviewnet.com/translation_of_interview_with_dr%20ayman%20al%20zawaahri.htm. Other jihadis agree on this relationship between the United States and Israel. See Siddiqi, *The Revival of the Muslim Ummah,* 5.

59. A concept agreed to by other jihadis. See Sheikh Safar Al-Hawali, "Open Letter to President Bush."

60. Osama Bin Laden, "On the Crusader War and the United Nations," 3

November 2002, http://www.jihadunspun.com/BinLadensNetwork/
statements/ootcwatun.cfm.

61. Ruhollah Khomeini, "The Granting of Capitulatory Rights to the
U.S. [October 27, 1964]," in *Islam and Revolution* (Berkeley: Mizan
Press, 1981), 187.

62. "Israeli-Zionist Army; A Long History of Murder and Terrorism," *Al-
Jihaad*, no. 0000.

63. Ziad Abu-Amr, *Islamic Fundamentalism in the West Bank and Gaza.
Muslim Brotherhood and Islamic Jihad* (Bloomington IN: Indiana University Press, 1994), 61; "Be Afraid, Be Very Afraid.

64. "A Statement from Al-Qaida to the Islamic Umma, on the First
Anniversary of the New American Crusader War," http://www.
jihadunspun.net/articles/10152002-To.The.Islamic.Ummah/
faotnacwo1.html; PBS *Frontline*, "Who Is Osama Bin Laden?" May
1998, http://www.jihadunspun.com/BinLadensNetwork/interviews/
pbsfrontline 05–1998.cfm; "The Religious Roots of the Upcoming
U.S. War," *Nida'ul Islam* 10, no. 1 (January/March 2003); discussed
also by Esther Webman, *Anti-Semitic Motifs in the Ideology of Hizballah
and Hamas* (Tel-Aviv: Tel-Aviv University, 1994), 25.

65. Sulayman Bin Jassem Abu Gheith, "Abu Gheith Speaks on Revisiting
Kenya," source Jehad Online, trans. Jihad Unspun, 7 December 7
2002, http://www.jihadunspun.net/BinLadensNetwork/statements/
agok.cfm; Abid Mustafa, "Roadmap Aims to Strengthen Israel and
Facilitate U.S. Grip over the Region," *Khilafah Magazine* (June 2003):
8–10; "Crusades Against Innocent Muslim Children In Iraq; Where
Are the Mujahidin?" *Al-Jihaad*, no. 3.

66. See, e.g., [Hamas], "The Covenant of the Islamic Resistance Movement (Hamas)," especially articles 22, 28, 32 and 34, 18 August 1988,
http://www.mideastweb.org/hamas.htm; [Hizb ut-Tahrir], "The Muslim Ummah Will Never Submit to the Jews," 3 November 1999,
http://www.hizb-ut-tahrir.org/english/leaflets/palestine31199.htm;

"U.S. & Britain; Supports Zionist-Israeli Terrorism; U.S. Involvement with the Disease Known as Israel," *Al-Jihaad*, no. oooo.

67. [Hizb ut-Tahrir], *The Inevitability of the Clash of Civilization*, 36–41.

68. By this jihadis mean the mindset, and thus correct behavior, that Islam creates in the true believer.

69. Emmanuel Sivan, *Radical Islam. Medieval Theology and Modern Politics* (New Haven: Yale University Press, 1985), 3–6.

70. Qutb, *In the Shade of the Qur'an*, vol. 6, 283–284; Amrozi, the "Bali bomber," said that the bombing "served whites right" because "they know how to destroy religions using the most subtle ways through bars, gambling dens. And you must realize the debauchery of their television." "Bali Bomb Suspect Says 'Served Whites Right'; 12 June 2003," http://news.yahoo.com/news?tmpl=story2&cid=586&u=/nm/20030612/wl_nm/indonesia_bali_dc&printer=1. This belief is not confined to the jihadis only, but is a common complaint by Islamists, who also see this as part of an insidious plot by the unbelievers to destroy Islam. Sheikh 'Abdul-'Aziz ibn Baz, "The Ideological Attack," *As-Sahar al-Islamiyah* (14 November 2000); Sheikh Muhammad Al-'Uthaymeen, "The Jews and Their Treachery," http://www.islamicawakening.com/viewarticle.php?articleID=940&.

71. Jamaaluddin al-Haidar, al-Bayan Chief Editor, "Reigns of Power," http://www.ummah.net.pk/albayan/fset2.html.

72. "Bin Laden Audio Released," 3 March 2004, http://www.homelandsecurityus.com/encyclopedia.asp.

73. Interview with Amir of the Mujahideen Party, Salahuddin, "The People of Kashmir Are Determined to Continue the Jihad Regardless of the Price," http://islam.org.au.

74. ALM Pakistan branch, "The Wishes and Tools of the Kufaar," 24 March 2003, http://homepage.ntlworld.com/mohammed.butt1/sitefiles/short-articles/kafir-unitied-nations-plans-1.htm.

75. "Integration—Al-Indimaaj," *As-Sahwa*, November 2001, 10; [Hizb

ut-Tahrir], *Dangerous Concepts*, 13–27; Jamaaluddin al-Haidar, al-Bayan Chief Editor, "Where from Here?" *al-Bayan*.

76. Sheikh Ali 'Abdur Rahmaan Hudhayfi, "Historic Khutbah"; Mufti Khubiab Sahib, *Zaad e Mujahid*, 45; [Hizb ut-Tahrir], *The Inevitability of the Clash of Civilization*, 36; OBM, "The Humiliation of Muslims by America: U.S. Expansionist," *Islamic Spotlight*, no. 26.

77. "The Media Onslaught," *As-Sahwa*, November 2001, 4–5; [Hizb ut-Tahrir], "The Campaign to Subvert Islam as an Ideology and a System"; Siddiqi, *Methodology of Dawah il Allah in American Perspective*, viii.

78. [Hizb ut-Tahrir], *The American Campaign to Suppress Islam*, 11.

79. "Farewell Message from Azzam Publications"; Sahib, *Zaad e Mujahid*, 45; [Hizb ut-Tahrir], *Dangerous Concepts*, 33–37; [Hizb ut-Tahrir], *The Inevitability of the Clash of Civilization*, 45; bin Laden, "On the Crusader War and the United Nations."

80. Siddiqi, *The Revival of the Muslim Ummah*; Safar bin 'Abdir-Rahmaan al-Hawaali, "A Statement To The Ummah Concerning the Recent Events," http://www.islamicawakening.com/index.htm? (http://www.as-sahwah.com/Articles/bayaan6.phtml); [Hizb ut-Tahrir], *Dangerous Concepts*, 8–12.

81. "Mujahid Usamah Bin Ladin Talks Exclusively to 'Nida'ul Islam'"; PBS *Frontline*, "Who Is Osama Bin Laden?" May 1998, http://www.jihadunspun.com/BinLadensNetwork/interviews/pbsfrontline05–1998.cfm.

82. Allouni, "The Unreleased Interview, 21 October 2001"; also, "Osama Bin Laden's Latest Statement," http://www.jihadunspun.net/BinLadensNetwork/statements/oblls.cfm.

83. For the Wahhabi view of U.S. educational reform efforts see "We, the Saudi People, Speak," http://www.boycottusa.org/articles_saudipeople.htm.

84. See, e.g., "Attacks from Within: Attempts to Destroy the Islamic

'Aqeedah," 20 July 1998, www.khalifornia.org; Amir interview, "The People of Kashmir Are Determined to Continue the Jihad Regardless of the Price."

85. Umayra, "The Destruction of the Khilafah: The Mother of All Crimes."

86. "Statement by al-Qaida."

87. OBM Network, "Our Relationship with Our Rulers and Scholars," http://www.gzastorm.i12.com/otherarticles/index.html.

88. Abu Hamza al-Masri, *The Need for Shari'a* (Supporters of Shari'ah); "Be Afraid, Be Very Afraid"; "Treachery from the Peninsula; Government Scholars Destroying Islam," *Al-Jihaad*, no. 4; "The Wishes and Tools of the Kufaar."

89. For descriptions of the European/American/Zionist/Crusader military war on Islam see "ABC Interview with Osama bin Laden"; Allouni with Usamah bin Laden, "The Unreleased Interview, 21 October 2001"; "Osama Bin Laden's Latest Statement"; bin Laden, "On the Crusader War and the United Nations"; "Statement by al-Qaida"; al-Hawaali, "A Statement to the Ummah Concerning the Recent Events"; Siddiqi, *The Revival of the Muslim Ummah*, 4–5; [Hizb ut-Tahrir], "Western States Slaughter the Muslims in the Balkans," 5 April 1999, http://www.hizb-ut-tahrir.org/english/leaflets/april0599.htm; "Qiyam ul Lail: The Battle of Badr Compared to the Battle for Chechnya," www.shu.ac.uk; Hani Jamal Eldin, "March 3rd 1924," *Khilafah Magazine* (March 2003): 8–10; [Hizb ut-Tahrir], "George Bush's Third Crusade Against the Muslims," 20 April 2002, http://www.mindspring.eu.com/thirdcrusade.htm.

90. "Mujahid Usamah Bin Ladin Talks Exclusively to 'Nida'ul Islam'"; "Bin Laadin Speaks on Hijrah; And the Islamic Emirate of Afghanistan," *Al-Jihaad*, no. 4.

91. World Islamic Front Statement, "Jihad Against Jews and Crusaders," 23 February 1998.

92. For a sense of the enormity of the campaign the jihadis believe they face, see Qutb, *In the Shade of the Qur'an*, vol. 4, 144; Qutb, *In the Shade of the Qur'an*, vol. 6, 238; "Two Camps: It Is Quite Clear That Their [*sic*] Are Two Camps Amongst the Muslims Worldwide. Which Camp Are You In?" http://homepage.ntlworld.com/ mohammed.butt1/ sitefiles/two_camps.htm; "Statement of Purpose," http://www .islamic-truth.fsnet.co.uk/; Siddiqi, *Methodology of Dawah il Allah in American Perspective*, viii; Mufti Khubiab Sahib, *Zaad e Mujahid*, 4–5, 11–12; Masood Azhar, *The Virtues of Jihad*, 132; Hudhayfi, "Historic Khutbah." The World Bank, IMF, and United Nations are hated by jihadis, who see them as tools for America's war on Islam. Osama Bin Laden, "On the Crusader War and the United Nations," http://www .jihadunspun.com/BinLadensNetwork/statements/ootcwatun.cfm; "Afghanistan Is Not an Islamic State," http://www.islamic-state.org/ afghanistan/; OBM, "The Humiliation of Muslims by America: U.S. Expansionist"; Ahmed Feroze, "The New Form of Colonialism and the Dangers to the Muslim Ummah," *Khilafah Magazine* (December 2000).

93. Qutb, *In the Shade of the Qur'an*, vol. 5, 312.

94. Every statement made by Usama bin Ladin confirms this is true for al-Qaida. For other groups, see [Hizb ut-Tahrir], "Destroy the Fourth Crusader War," 20 March 2003, n.p.; Haydar Ali Khan, "A Shift in Relations Between America & Saudi Arabia," *Khilafah Magazine* 15, no. 3 (March 2002): 11–12; Asim Khan, "The Secularists Jihad," *Khilafah Magazine* 15, no. 3 (March 2002): 18; [Hizb ut-Tahrir], *The American Campaign to Suppress Islam*, [throughout]; "The Humiliation of Muslims by America. The International Struggle over Africa Intensified," www.obm.clara.net/new/usa5.html.

95. "Western Justice—Where the Scales Remain Unbalanced," *As-Sahwa*, November 2001, 9.

6. *The Clash of Civilizations, Part II*

1. This discussion is taken from Ahmad ibn Lu'lu' ibn al-Naqib al-Misri, *The Reliance of the Traveller,* ['*Umdat al-sÇlik wa-'uddat al-nÇsik*] ed. and trans. Noah Ha Mim Keller (Evanston, IL: Sunna Books, 1991), parts O 9.0–O 9.9.

2. See, e.g., A. G. Noorani, *Islam & Jihad. Prejudice Versus Reality* (London: Zed Books, 2002), 45–56; Khaled Abou El Fadl, *The Place of Tolerance in Islam* (Boston: Beacon Press, 2002), 19; John L. Esposito, "Struggle in Islam," in Khaled Abou El Fadl, *The Place of Tolerance in Islam,* 76.

3. Qur'an 5:35; Qur'an 22:78; Qur'an 29:6; Qur'an 29:69; Qur'an 49:15; Qur'an 61:11.

4. See Qur'an 25:52—"Therefore listen not to the Unbelievers, but strive against them with the utmost strenuousness, with the (Qur'an)."

5. E.g., Qur'an 47:31—"And verily We shall try you till We know those of you who strive hard (for the cause of Allah) [mujahidun] and the steadfast, and till We test your record."

6. Johannes J. G. Jansen, *The Neglected Duty. The Creed of Sadat's Assassins and Islamic Resurgence in the Middle East* (New York: Macmillan, 1986), 201; Abu Fadl, "Greater and Lesser Jihad," *Nida'ul Islam,* no. 26 (April–May 1999); Asim Khan, "The Secularists Jihad," *Khilafah Magazine* 15, no. 3 (March 2002): 17; Sidik Aucbur, "The True Meaning of Jihad," *Khilafah Magazine* (May 2003): 17–18.

7. See, e.g., Moulana Mohammed Masood Azhar, *The Virtues of Jihad* [*Ahle Sunnah Wal Jama'at*], n.p., n.d., 6.

8. "Bin Laadin Speaks on Hijrah; And the Islamic Emirate of Afghanistan," *Al-Jihaad,* no. 4; Rashid Ali, "Jihad: The Highest Peak of Islam," *Khilafah Magazine* (December 2001); Fathi Yakan, *To Be a Muslim,* n.p., n.d.; The term *jihad* is the "peak of the religion" is taken from al-Tirmidhi's hadith and is not found in the "two sahihs," the most respected collections of hadith.

9. Abul A'la Maududi, *Jihad in Islam [Jihad fi Sabil Allah]* (Lagos: Ibrash Islamic Publications Centre, 1939), 18.

10. A point also made in Mehdi Abedi and Gary Legenhausen, "Introduction," in Mehdi Abedi and Gary Legenhausen, eds., *Jihad and* Shahadat. *Struggle and Martyrdom in Islam* (Houston: Institute for Research and Islamic Studies, 1986), 15.

11. Maududi, *Jihad in Islam*, 23.

12. Sayyid Qutb, Milestones (Delhi: Markazi Maktaba Islami, 1991), 111.

13. Fathi Yakan, *To Be a Muslim.*

14. [Hizb ut-Tahrir], *The Inevitability of the Clash of Civilization* (London: Al-Khilafah, 2002), 36–46.

15. "ABC Interview with Osama bin Laden," January 1998, http://www .jihadunspun.net/BinLadensNetwork/interviews/abc01–1998.cfm.

16. See Qur'an 2:217, 16:41.

17. Sayyid Qutb, *In the Shade of the Qur'an [Fi Zilal al-Qur'an]*, vol. 1 (Markfield, Leicester: The Islamic Foundation, 1999), 208–209; Sayyid Qutb, *In the Shade of the Qur'an [Fi Zilal al-Qur'an]*, vol. 7 (Markfield, Leicester: The Islamic Foundation, 2003), 134; [Hizb ut-Tahrir], "And Kill Them Wherever You Find Them, and Turn Them Out from Where They Have Turned You Out," 31 March 2002, http://www.islamic-state.org/leaflets/020331_AndKillThem WhereeverYouFindThem.php; "Mujahid Usamah Bin Ladin Talks Exclusively to "Nida'ul Islam" About the New Powder Keg in the Middle East," *Nida'ul Islam*, no. 15 (October/November 1996); World Islamic Front statement, "Jihad Against Jews and Crusaders," 23 February 1998; "Statement by al-Qaida," *The Observer*, 24 November 2002.

18. See, e.g., Yousef Al-Qaradawi, *Priorities of the Islamic Movement in the Coming Phase* (Cairo: Dar al Nashr, 1992), 176–181.

19. [Hizb al-Tahrir], "Hizb-ut-Tahrir," http://www.hizb-ut-tahrir.org/english/.

20. 'Usama Bin Muhammad Bin Ladin, "Declaration of War Against the Americans Occupying the Land of the Two Holy Places (Expel the Infidels from the Arab Peninsula)," *The Idler* 3, no. 165 (13 September 2001). Hizb al-Tahrir described the first Gulf War in the same terms, dismissing the arguments about Iraq's aggression as a mere excuse to invade and occupy Kuwait and Arabia and begin exploiting their oil resources. [Hizb ut-Tahrir], *The Inevitability of the Clash of Civilization* (London: Al-Khilafah, 2002), 42.

21. Omar Bakri Muhammad, "The Islamic Verdict on: Jihad and the Method to Establish the Khilafah," http://www.geocities.com/al-khilafah/JIHAD2.htm, 17.

22. See [Hamas], "The Covenant of the Islamic Resistance Movement (Hamas)," article 7, 18 August 1988, http://www.mideastweb.org/hamas.htm. This is also the view of some Islamists. See Yousef Qaradhawi, "Speech Before the 11th Session of the European Council for Fatwa and Research," 19 July 2003. *MEMRI Special Dispatch—Jihad and Terrorism Studies Project*, Middle East Media Research Institute, no. 542, 24 July 2003, http://www.MEMRI/bin/opener_latest.cgi?ID=SD54203.

23. Interview with Amir of the Mujahideen Party, Salahuddin, "The People of Kashmir Are Determined to Continue the Jihad Regardless of the Price," http://islam.org.au.

24. Quoted in Al-Qaradawi, *Priorities of the Islamic Movement*, 178.

25. 'Abdullah 'Azzam, *Defense of the Muslim Lands. The First Obligation After Iman.* n.p., n.d. For his beliefs about Spain, Bulgaria, and elsewhere see 'Abdullah 'Azzam, *Join the Caravan*, 2d ed. (n.p., 1988).

26. Sheikh Safar Al-Hawali, "Open Letter to President Bush," 15 October 2001, http://www.muslimuzbekistan.com/eng/ennews/2001/10/ennews20102001.html.

27. http://www.iberiannotes.blogspot.com/2004_04_11_iberiannotes_archive.html#108193744360327580.

28. [Hizb ut-Tahrir], "Western States Slaughter the Muslims in the Balkans," 5 April 1999, http://www.hizb-ut-tahrir.org/english/leaflets/april0599.htm.

29. Hafiz Abdul Salam Bin Muhammad, *Jihad in the Present Time* [*Jihaad ul-Kuffaari wal-Munaafiqeen*], http://www.tamibooks.com/data2/jihad.html.

30. "Qiyam ul Lail: The Battle of Badr Compared to the Battle for Chechnya," www.shu.ac.uk. Of course, these maximalist wish lists show only what jihadist groups would like eventually to achieve and do not say anything about where precisely they will decide to carry out their next attacks. The following chapter addresses how some groups have prioritized their lists of enemies and where they are likely to attack.

31. 'Abdullah 'Azzam, *Defense of the Muslim Lands*.

32. For a discussion of this issue by a respected Islamic scholar see Shaikh Abdullah Ghoshah, "The Jihad Is the Way to Gain Victory," Academy of Islamic Research, Al Azhar, *The Fourth Conference of the Academy of Islamic Research* (Cairo: General Organization of Government Printing Offices, 1968), 179–250.

33. Qutb, *Milestones*, 102.

34. Qutb, *In the Shade of the Qur'an*, vol. 1, 328.

35. Khubiab Sahib, *Zaad e Mujahid* [*Essential Provision of the Mujahid*], n.p., n.d., 40.

36. Sidik Aucbur, "The True Meaning of Jihad," *Khilafah Magazine* (May 2003): 17–18; Moulana Mohammed Masood Azhar, *The Virtues of Jihad* [Ahle Sunnah Wal Jama'at], n.p., n.d., 12; "Jihad in the Quran; 'Jihad Is Prescribed For You,'" *Al-Jihaad*, no. 10, http://www.shareeah.com/Eng/aj/aj10.html; Omar Bakri Muhammad, "The Islamic Verdict on: Jihad and the Method to Establish the Khilafah," 5.

37. Sahib, *Zaad e Mujahid*, 23, 26; Azhar, *The Virtues of Jihad*, 53.

38. Hasan al-Banna, "To What Do We Summon Mankind?" in *Five Tracts*

of Hasan Al-Banna. A Selection from the Majmu 'at Rasa'il al-Imam al-Shahid Hasan al-Banna,' trans. Charles Wendell (Berkeley: University of California Press, 1978), 80–81; Hasan al-Banna, "On Jihad," in ibid., 142, 150; Qutb, *In the Shade of the Qur'an*, vol. 7, 131; Muhammad, *The Islamic Verdict on: Jihad*, 7–10; Shaikh Abdur-Rahmaan Abdul-Khaaliq, *The Islamic Ruling on The Peace Process*, n.p., n.d.; 'Azzam, *Join The Caravan;* [Hizb ut-Tahrir], "A Draft Constitution," *The System of Islam*, article 56; Jamaal al-ddin Zarabozo, "The Importance of Jihad in the Life of a Muslim," *Al-Bashir Magazine*, http://groups.yahoo.com/group/algeriaonline/message/315; Jansen, *The Neglected Duty*, 195–196.

39. Also called *kalima*, the other term for the shahada.
40. Maududi, *Jihad in Islam*, 16; Sahib, *Zaad e Mujahid*, 11–12.
41. Sheikh 'Usama Bin Muhammad Bin Ladin, "Declaration of War Against the Americans Occupying the Land of the Two Holy Places (Expel the Infidels from the Arab Peninsula)," *The Idler* 3, no. 165 (13 September 2001).
42. "ABC Interview with Osama bin Laden," January 1998, http://www.jihadunspun.net/BinLadensNetwork/interviews/abc01–1998.cfm; "Osama Bin Laden's Latest Statement," http://www.jihadunspun.net/BinLadensNetwork/statements/oblls.cfm.
43. The term used for "opening" (*fath*) is so associated with fighting that it now also means "conquest" in ordinary Arabic. "To open a country" thus has come to mean "to conquer a country [for Islam]."
44. William E. Shepard, *Sayyid Qutb and Islamic Activism: A Translation and Critical Analysis of Social Justice in Islam* (New York: E. J. Brill, 1996), 213–214.
45. Rashid Ali, "Jihad: The Highest Peak of Islam," *Khilafah Magazine* (December 2001).
46. Al-Banna, "To What Do We Summon Mankind?" 80–81.
47. *fitna.*

48. Quoted in Yakan, *To Be a Muslim.*

49. Maududi, *Jihad in Islam,* 4–6.

50. Qutb, *In the Shade of the Qur'an,* vol. 7, 135, 150. See also Qutb, *Milestones,* 93–140.

51. Qutb, *Milestones,* 113–114.

52. Qutb, *In the Shade of the Qur'an,* vol. 7, 22.

53. OBM Network, "Treaties in Islam," n.d.; "Bin Laadin Speaks on Hijrah."

54. See Abdur-Rahmaan Abdul-Khaaliq, *The Islamic Ruling on the Peace Process;* Omar Bakri Mohammad, *Jihad: The Foreign Policy of the Islamic State,* n.p., n.d.; Muhammad, *The Islamic Verdict on: Jihad,* 10–11; [Hizb ut-Tahrir], *The Methodology of Hizb ut-Tahrir for Change* (London: Al-Khilafah Publications, 1999), 10, 24; Sahib, *Zaad e Mujahid,* 75; Jamaal al-ddin Zarabozo, "The Importance of Jihad in the Life of a Muslim"; Shaykh Abu Muhammad al-Maqdisi (Shaykh 'Isam al-Burqawi), *This Is Our Aqidah!* n.p., n.d.

55. Qutb, *In the Shade of the Qur'an,* vol. 1, 208; Sayyid Qutb, *In the Shade of the Qur'an [Fi Zilal al-Qur'an],* vol. 2 (Markfield, Leicester: The Islamic Foundation, 2000), 170–173; Shaikh Abdur-Rahmaan Abdul-Khaaliq, *The Islamic Ruling on the Peace Process;* Azhar, *The Virtues of Jihad,* 103; [Hizb-ut-Tahrir], "The Muslim Ummah Will Never Submit to the Jews," 3 November 1999, http://www.hizb-ut-tahrir.org/ english/leaflets/palestine31199.htm; Abu Hamza al-Masri, *What Is Wrong. The Way to Get Shari'a* (Supporters of Shari'a); 'Issam Amireh (Abu Abdullah), "Signs of the Impending Victory" (speech, University of al-Quds, 9 December 2001), http://www.khilafah.com/home/ lographics/category.php?DocumentID=1023&TagID=24. The corollary to this is that Muslims cannot allow the unbelievers to usurp the rightful authority of Islam or to dominate anywhere on the earth. See 'Abdullah 'Azzam, "Reasons for Jihad," in *Join The Caravan.*

56. The *lex talionis* and supporting texts are Qur'an 5:45 and 2:178–179.

Support for aggressing against an enemy as he aggresses against the believers is taken from Qur'an 2:194 and 16:126.

57. World Islamic Front Statement, "Jihad Against Jews and Crusaders," 23 February 1998.

58. Sheikh Hammoud Al-Uqlaa Ash-Shuaybi, "Fatwa on Events Following 11 September 2001," http://perso.wanadoo.fr/centralparkattacks/islam.html.

59. Safar bin 'Abdir-Rahmaan al-Hawaali, "A Statement to the Ummah Concerning the Recent Events," http://www.islamicawakening.com/index.htm? (http://www.as-sahwah.com/Articles/bayaan6.phtml).

60. Osama bin Muhammad bin Laden, "A Message to the American People," trans. Jihad Unspun, 7 October 2002, http://www.jihadunspun.com/BinLadensNetwork/statements/amta.html.

61. Tayseer Allouni with Usamah bin Laden, "The Unreleased Interview, 21 October 2001," from Markaz Derasat (translated by Muawiya ibn Abi Sufyan), http://www.islamicawakening.com/index.htm? (http://www.as-sahwah.com).

62. Azzam Publications, "Translation of Interview with Dr. Ayman al Zawaahri," September 2002, http://www.mediareviewnet.com/translation_of_interview_with_dr%20ayman%20al%20zawaahri.htm.

63. Azhar, *The Virtues of Jihad*, 67; Jansen, *The Neglected Duty*, 210–215.

64. *Sahih Bukhari*, vol. 4, Book 52, nos. 267, 268, 269; *Sahih Muslim*, book 19, nos. 4311, 4312; *Abu Sunan Dawud*, book 14, no. 2631.

65. Abu'l-Hasan 'Ali ibn Muhammad ibn Habib al-Basri al-Baghdadi al Mawardi, *Al-Ahkam as-Sultaniyyah: The Laws of Islamic Governance*, trans. Asadullah Yate (London: Ta-Ha Publishers, 1996), 64. See also Jansen, *The Neglected Duty*, 215–216.

66. See Sheikh Muhammad Sayed al-Tantawi, head of al-Azhar, quoted in *Al-Wafd*, 27 April 1996, and in *Al Shab*, 4 April 1996, and Muhsin al-Awaji, a Saudi lawyer prominent in religious affairs, in "We, the Saudi People, Speak," http://www.boycottusa.org/articles_saudipeople.htm.

67. Khutbah of 9 June 2000, delivered at Finsbury Park Mosque by Sheikh Abu Hamza, "She Died a Mujaahida; Killing 27 Russian Soldiers," *Al-Jihaad*, no. 4; [Hizb ut-Tahrir], "And Kill Them Wherever You Find Them, and Turn Them Out from Where They Have Turned You Out," 31 March 2002, http://www.islamic-state.org/leaflets/020331_And KillThemWhereeverYouFindThem.php; Azzam Publications, "Translation of Interview with Dr. Ayman al Zawaahri," September 2002.

68. For some examples of this see al Mawardi, *Al-Ahkam as-Sultaniyya*, 64–66; 'Abdullah ibn Abi Zayd al-Qayrawani, *The Risala: A Treatise on Maliki Fiqh (922–996)*, trans. Alhaj Bello Mohammad Daura, http://www2.iiu.edu.my/deed/lawbase/risalah_maliki/, 30.2h–30.2j; Sidi Khalil, *Mukhtasar (Maliki Law)*, trans. F. H. Lawton (Westport, CT: Hyperion, 1980), 74–77.

69. This discussion is taken from Khalil, *Mukhtasar (Maliki Law)*, 74–75; 'Abdullah ibn Abi Zayd al-Qayrawani, *The Risala*, 30.2i–30.2j; al Mawardi, *Al-Ahkam as-Sultaniyyah*, 64–65; al-Misri, *The Reliance of the Traveller*, O 9.10; Taqi ad-Din Ibn Taymiyyah, *Ibn Taymiyyah Expounds on Islam*, trans. Muhammad 'Abdul-Haqq Ansari (Riyadh: Imam Muhammad Ibn Saud University, 2000), 544.

70. Muhammad, "The Islamic Verdict on: Jihad"; 'Azzam, *Defense of the Muslim Lands*; Abu Hamza al-Masri, *What Is Wrong. The Way to Get Shari'a* (Supporters of Shari'a), 4–5; Jansen, *The Neglected Duty*, 217–218.

71. Jansen, *The Neglected Duty*, 207–209.

72. Interview with Hamid Mir, Editor of Ausaf, "Osama bin Laden Claims He Has Nukes," 9 November 2001, http://www.jihadunspun.com/BinLadensNetwork/interviews/index.cfm; Ash-Shuaybi, "Fatwa on Events Following 11 September 2001."

73. "ABC Interview with Osama bin Laden."

74. Mufti Khubiab Sahib, *Zaad e Mujahid*, 102–103; Report by Qaradhawi

at the 11th Session of the European Council for Fatwa and Research, published by Al-Sharq Al-Awsat, London, 19 July 2003. *MEMRI Special Dispatch—Jihad and Terrorism Studies Project*, Middle East Media Research Institute, no. 542, 24 July 2003.

75. Ash-Shuaybi, "Fatwa on Events Following 11 September 2001."

76. al Mawardi, *Al-Ahkam as-Sultaniyyah*, 76, 192–193; al-Qayrawani, *The Risala*, 30.2h; Khalil, *Mukhtasar (Maliki Law)*, 77; al-Misri, *The Reliance of the Traveller*, O 9.14.

77. See the lengthy legal justifications given in the jihadist explanation about killing Russian prisoners in Chechnya: "The Islamic Ruling on the Permissibility of Executing Prisoners of War," www.qoqaz.net.

78. Mohammad Shehzad, "Top Jihadi Says Musharraf Is a Traitor: Jihad Will Continue," http://www.satribune.com/archives/aug24_30_03/P1_azhar.htm.

79. They also reason that a) nonbelieving governments torture Muslims, b) this is a good way to obtain information, and c) this "is a form of necessary punishment." For all these reasons, they recommend kidnapping, interrogating, and torturing enemy personnel for intelligence. "Declaration of Jihad Against the Country's Tyrants" (al-Qaida manual), 81, 95–96, http://web.tiscali.it/unitedstates/articles.htm.

80. al Mawardi, *Al-Ahkam as-Sultaniyyah*, 78.

81. Khalil, *Mukhtasar (Maliki Law)*, 85. One of the major treatises of Shafi'i law does not even mention the possibility of truces, peace treaties, or other agreements with non-Muslims. See al-Misri, *The Reliance of the Traveller*, O 9.16.

82. 'Azzam, *Defense of the Muslim Land*; Asif Khan, "Treaties in Islam," *Khilafah Magazine* (July 2003): 27–30.

83. Sayyid Qutb, *This Religion of Islam* [*Hadha 'd-din*] (Palo Alto, CA: Al-Manar, 1967), 90 (emphasis mine).

84. Muhammad, "The Islamic Verdict on: Jihad," 10–11; Sheikh Omar Bakri Muhammad, "Is Peace with Israel Possible?: The Islamic Ver-

dict," *al-Bayan*; OBM Network, "Treaties in Islam," n.p., n.d.;
[Hamas], "The Covenant of the Islamic Resistance Movement
(Hamas)," article 13, 18 August 1988, http://www.mideastweb.org/
hamas.htm.

85. [Hizb ut-Tahrir], "A Draft Constitution: Articles 186, 187"; Abdul-
Khaaliq, *The Islamic Ruling on the Peace Process*; Abu Sumaya, "Editorial," *Al-Jihaad*, no. 0000.

86. See, e.g., Qur'an 48:19–20; *Sahih Bukhari*, vol. 4, Book 52, is full of
references to booty, as is Book 53 (which is dedicated to how to divide
the booty) and Book 59 (on the military expeditions of Muhammad).
The other hadith collections are similarly replete with references to
booty.

87. al Mawardi, *Al-Ahkam as-Asultaniyya*, 76, 186–206; al-Qayrawani, *The
Risala*, 30.3–30.4; Khalil, *Mukhtasar (Maliki Law)*, 75–82; al-Misri,
The Reliance of the Traveller, O 10.0.

88. 'Azzam, *Join the Caravan*; Jansen, *The Neglected Duty*, 177; Sahib, *Zaad
e Mujahid*, 91.

89. Azhar, *The Virtues of Jihad*, 101.

90. [Hizb ut-Tahrir], "A Draft Constitution, Article 145," *The System of
Islam*.

91. 'Usama Bin Muhammad Bin Ladin, "Declaration of War Against the
Americans Occupying the Land of the Two Holy Places (Expel the
Infidels from the Arab Peninsula)," *The Idler* 3, no. 165 (13 September
2001).

92. World Islamic Front Statement, "Jihad Against Jews and Crusaders,"
23 February 1998.

93. Qur'an 8:60.

94. *Sahih Bukhari*, vol. 52, Book 4, no. 220; *Sahih Muslim*, Book 4, nos.
1062–1067.

95. Qutb, *In the Shade of the Qur'an*, vol. 7, 186.

96. Khutbah of 9 June 2000, delivered at Finsbury Park Mosque by Sheikh

Abu Hamza, "She Died a Mujaahida; Killing 27 Russian Soldiers," *Al-Jihaad*, no. 4.

97. PBS Frontline, "Who Is Osama Bin Laden?" May 1998, http://www.jihadunspun.com/BinLadensNetwork/interviews/ pbsfrontline05–1998.cfm.

98. 'Usama Bin Muhammad Bin Ladin, "Declaration of War"; Abu Ghaith, "Statement," 10 October 2001, http://news.bbc.co.uk/2/hi/ middle_east/1590350.stm.

99. "We, the Saudi People, Speak," http://www.boycottusa.org/ articles_saudipeople.htm.

7. *From Mecca to Medina*

1. Literally, "[course of one's] life," "biography."

2. Kalim Siddiqui, "Political Dimensions of the Seerah," *ICIT Papers on the Seerah* (The Institute of Contemporary Islamic Thought), 9–10.

3. [No author], "The Meaning of Seerah," in Iyad Hilal, ed., *Selections from the Seerah of Muhammad* (London: Khilafah Publications, n.d.), 7–8; Iyad Hilal, "Usul al-Fiqh: The Authority of Sunnah," in ibid., 25–31.

4. [No author], "The Seerah of the Messenger (Saw)" (translated from *Al-Waie Magazine*), *Khilafah Magazine* (January 2001).

5. Quoted in Fathi Yakan, *To Be a Muslim*, n.p., n.d.

6. The discussion following is taken from Sayyid Qutb, *In the Shade of the Qur'an [Fi Zilal al-Qur'an]*, vol. 1 (Markfield, Leicester: The Islamic Foundation, 1999), 11–15, 206–208; Sayyid Qutb, *In the Shade of the Qur'an [Fi Zilal al-Qur'an]*, vol. 3 (Markfield, Leicester: The Islamic Foundation, 2001), 228–236; Sayyid Qutb, *In the Shade of the Qur'an [Fi Zilal al-Qur'an]*, vol. 5 (Markfield, Leicester: The Islamic Foundation, 2002), 11–19; Sayyid Qutb, *In the Shade of the Qur'an [Fi Zilal al-Qur'an]*, vol. 7 (Markfield, Leicester: The Islamic Foundation, 2003), 15–18, 148, 208–216; Sayyid Qutb, *In the Shade of the Qur'an [Fi Zilal al-Qur'an]*, vol. 8 (Markfield, Leicester: The Islamic Foundation, 2003),

23–24, 308ff; Sayyid Qutb, *Milestones* (Delhi: Markazi Maktaba Islami, 1991), 16–17, 32–33, 60–62, 84–85, 139–140, 147.

7. English "Hegira."

8. Even the Islamist Qaradhawi, for instance, disagrees with Qutb's views of strategic stages and the need for a modern hijra. See Yousef Al-Qaradawi, *Priorities of the Islamic Movement in the Coming Phase* (Cairo: Dar al Nashr, 1992), 173–175.

9. For a detailed description of Hizb al-Tahrir's vision of stages at its inception see Suha Taji-Farouki, *A Fundamental Quest. Hizb al-Tahrir and the Search for the Islamic Caliphate* (London: Grey Seal, 1996), 89–105. A much later and more developed version is presented in Imran Waheed, "How to Re-establish the Khilafah The Method of Muhammad (Saw)?" 27 August 2000, *Khilafah Magazine* (October 2000).

10. See, e.g., Muhammad Al-Asi, "The Unknown Prophet: Forgotten Dimensions of the Seerah," *ICIT Papers on the Seerah* (The Institute of Contemporary Islamic Thought); Kalim Siddiqui, "Political Dimensions of the Seerah," *ICIT Papers on the Seerah* (The Institute of Contemporary Islamic Thought); [Hizb ut-Tahrir], *The Methodology of Hizb ut-Tahrir for Change* (London: Al-Khilafah Publications, 1999), 13, 29.

11. Samir Dashi, "The Method of Changing the Society," in Iyad Hilal, ed., *Selections from the Seerah of Muhammad* (London: Khilafah Publications, n.d.), 65–66; [Hizb ut-Tahrir], *The Methodology of Hizb ut-Tahrir for Change*, 32ff; [No author], "The Seerah of the Messenger (Saw)" (translated from *Al-Waie Magazine*), *Khilafah Magazine* (January 2001).

12. Taji-Farouki, *A Fundamental Quest*, 79; Yakin, *To Be a Muslim*.

13. "A New Bin Laden Speech," 18 July 2003, Middle East Media Research Institute (hereafter MEMRI). These last two subphases are also part of the strategy suggested by Shamim Siddiqi, an American jihadi, who argued for the call to be combined with instruction (*tarbiyya*) and

purification (*tazkiyya*), which would train the elite vanguard group for their future work. Shamim A Siddiqi, *The Importance of Hijrah*, http://www.dawahinamericas.com/hijra.htm; and Shamim A. Siddiqi, *Methodology of Dawah il Allah in American Perspective* (New York: Forum for Islamic Work, 1989), 35–36.

14. Abul 'Ala Maudoodi, *The Process of Islamic Revolution*, 2d ed. (Lahore: Maktaba Jama'at-e-Islami Pakistan, 1955), 21, 30–31.

15. Maudoodi, *The Process of Islamic Revolution*, 49–52; Sayyid Qutb, *This Religion of Islam* [*Hadha 'd-din*] (Palo Alto, CA: Al-Manar, 1967), 6–10.

16. "The Way to Khilaafa; Following Verses Before Analogy," *Al-Jihaad*, no. 4; "Who Are the Ghurabaa'—The Strangers?" http://www.islamicawakening.com/index.htm? (http://www.as-sahwah.com); Sulayman Bin Jassem Abu Gheith, "Abu Gheith Speaks On Revisiting Kenya," source Jehad Online, translated by Jihad Unspun, 7 December 2002, http://www.jihadunspun.net/BinLadensNetwork/statements/agok.cfm.

17. Sheikh Omar Bakri Muhammad, *The Islamic Verdict on: Groups & Parties*, n.p., n.d.

18. Siddiqi, *Methodology of Dawah il Allah in American Perspective*, 15.

19. Taji-Farouki, *A Fundamental Quest*, 176.

20. See, e.g., "Some Statements of the Scholars Regarding Hijrah (Part 1)," in Shaikh Husayn Al-'Awayishah, *Al-Fasl-ul-Mubin fi Mas'alat-il-Hijrah wa Mufaraqat-il-Mushrikin*, trans. Isma'eel Alarcon (reprinted at al-manhaj.com).

21. The ahadith used by modern Islamic scholars to support their views are *Bukhari*, vol. 4, Book 52, nos. 42, 311–313; *Muslim*, Book 20, nos. 4594–4599.

22. For comparison, the more traditionally minded Islamic separatists in southern Thailand argue for the creation of an independent Islamic state as their place for hijra because they are oppressed by the majority Buddhist population. Peter Chalk, "Militant Islamic Separatism in

Southern Thailand," in *Islam in Asia. Changing Political Realities*, ed. Jason F. Isaacson and Colin Rubenstein (New Brunswick, NJ: Transaction Publishers, 2002), 165.

23. Siddiqi, *The Importance of Hijrah.*

24. Siddiqi, *Methodology of Dawah il Allah in American Perspective*, viii.

25. "Crusades Against Innocent Muslim Children in Iraq; Where Are the Mujahidin?" *Al-Jihaad*, no. 3, http://www.shareeah.com/Eng/aj/aj3.html; "Editorial," *Al-Jihaad*, no. 4.

26. "The Way to Khilaafa; Following Verses Before Analogy."

27. Asif Khan, "The Search for Nusrah," *Khilafah Magazine* 16, no. 1 (January 2003): 20.

28. "Understanding the Method of the Islamic Ideology," *Khilafah Magazine* (December 2000).

29. Abd us-Sami, "The Meaning of Hijrah," in Hilal, *Selections from the Seerah of Muhammad*, 76.

30. For discussions by Hizb al-Tahrir members of the nusra, see [Hizb ut-Tahrir], *The Methodology of Hizb ut-Tahrir for Change* (London: Al-Khilafah Publications, 1999), 37–40; "The Seerah of the Messenger (Saw)"; Khan, "The Search for Nusrah," 18–21. The only other jihadi to support Hizb al-Tahrir in their search for the nusra is 'Umar Bakri Muhammad of al-Muhajiroun, who has described this same method for winning over popular support and eventually power for the "true" Muslims. See, e.g., Omar Bakri Muhammad, "The Islamic Verdict on: Jihad and the Method to Establish the Khilafah," http://www.geocities.com/al-khilafah/JIHAD2.htm, 27.

31. Siddiqi, *Methodology of Dawah il Allah in American Perspective*, 44.

32. Gilles Kepel, *Muslim Extremism in Egypt. The Prophet and Pharaoh* (Berkeley: University of California Press, [1984] 2003), 75, 82.

33. "Afghanistan Return of Islam; Conference Held at Finsbury Park Mosque," *Al-Jihaad*, no. 3.

34. "Crusades Against Innocent Muslim Children in Iraq."

35. "Bin Laadin Speaks on Hijrah; And the Islamic Emirate of Afghanistan," *Al-Jihaad*, no. 4.

36. See ibid. as well as "ABC Interview with Osama bin Laden," January 1998, http://www.jihadunspun.net/BinLadensNetwork/interviews/ abc01–1998.cfm; Tayseer Allouni with Usamah bin Laden, "The Unreleased Interview, 21 October 2001," from Markaz Derasat (translated by Muawiya ibn Abi Sufyan), http://www.islamicawakening.com/ index.htm? (http://www.as-sahwah.com).

37. "ABC Interview with Osama bin Laden," January 1998, http://www .jihadunspun.net/BinLadensNetwork/interviews/abc01–1998.cfm.

38. "A New Bin Laden Speech," 18 July 2003, MEMRI. This also was the view of 'Abdullah 'Azzam, one of the major intellectual influences on bin Ladin and al-Qaida. 'Abdullah 'Azzam, *Join the Caravan*, 2d ed. (1988).

39. See, e.g., Samir Dashi, "The Method of Changing the Society," in Hilal, *Selections from the Seerah of Muhammad*, 68.

40. Kalim Siddiqui, "Political Dimensions of the Seerah," *ICIT Papers on the Seerah* (The Institute of Contemporary Islamic Thought).

41. *Sultan*, also called security (*'aman*).

42. "The Way to Khilaafa; Following Verses Before Analogy"; Muhammad, *The Islamic Verdict on: Jihad*, 26; [Hizb ut-Tahrir], *The Methodology of Hizb ut-Tahrir for Change* (London: Al-Khilafah Publications, 1999), 8–14; Jansen, *The Neglected Duty*, 165–166; "Bin Laadin Speaks on Hijrah; And The Islamic Emirate of Afghanistan." Hizb al-Tahrir has argued, from the fact that these criteria were never met, that Afghanistan was not the coming Khilafa. "Afghanistan Is Not an Islamic State," http://www.islamic-state.org/afghanistan/.

43. [Hizb ut-Tahrir], "A Draft Constitution," in [Hizb ut-Tahrir], *The System of Islam*, n.p., n.d.

44. See, e.g., "The Foreign Policy," www.shu.ac.uk; Muhammad, *The Islamic Verdict on: Jihad*, 5.

45. ʿIssam Amireh (Abu Abdullah), "Signs of the Impending Victory" (speech, University of al-Quds, 12 September 2001), http://www.khilafah.com/home/lographics/category.php?DocumentID=1023&TagID=24.

46. Azzam Publications, "Translation of Interview with Dr. Ayman al Zawaahri," September 2002, http://www.mediareviewnet.com/translation_of_interview_with_dr%20ayman%20al%20zawaahri.htm.

47. See, e.g., Mufti Khubiab Sahib, *Zaad e Mujahid* [*Essential Provision of the Mujahid*], n.p., n.d, 20.

48. "A New Bin Laden Speech.".

49. ʿAzzam, *Join The Caravan.*

50. Muhammad, *The Islamic Verdict on: Jihad,* 27.

51. ʿUmar Bakri Muhammad was a member of Hizb al-Tahrir until he split from them in 1983 to form al-Muhajiroun.

52. "Text of a Defence Speech Given by Wali Yildarem on 26/6/2002 Before the Second State Security Court in Adanah Regarding the Issue of Hizb ut-Tahrir," http://www.islamic-state.org/leaflets/murafa1.htm; "Text of a Defence Speech Given by Zaki Jeshkin on 26/6/2002 Before the Second State Security Court in Adanah Regarding the Issue of Hizb ut-Tahrir," http://www.hizb-ut-tahrir.info/english/dawah_news/2002/murafa2.htm.

53. See, e.g., [Hizb ut-Tahrir], "The Muslim Ummah Will Never Submit to the Jews," 3 November 1999, http://www.hizb-ut-tahrir.org/english/leaflets/palestine31199.htm.

54. Quoted in ʿUsama Bin Muhammad Bin Ladin, "Declaration of War Against the Americans Occupying the Land of the Two Holy Places (Expel the Infidels from the Arab Peninsula)," *The Idler* 3, no. 165 (13 September 2001). Also much quoted by other jihadis; see, e.g., Jamaaluddin al-Haidar, al-Bayan Chief Editor, "Where from Here?" *al-Bayan,* http://web.archive.org/web/20021203123657/www.ummah.net/albayan/fset2.html. The word used for "unbelief" here is kufr.

55. For the use by al-Qaida—and especially bin Ladin—of the term "main/greater unbelief," and their argument against being distracted from this primary task, see "ABC Interview with Osama bin Laden"; Sheikh 'Usama Bin Muhammad Bin Ladin, "Declaration of War Against the Americans"; Sulayman Bin Jassem Abu Gheith, "Abu Gheith Speaks on Revisiting Kenya"; Jamaaluddin al-Haidar "Where From Here?"

56. See, e.g., Mark Huband, *Warriors of the Prophet. The Struggle for Islam* (Boulder, CO: Westview Press, 1999), 115. Even some extremists within Hizb al-Tahrir have changed their focus from the agent-rulers to the United States as the main enemy, especially since the United States invaded Iraq. See [Hizb ut-Tahrir], "George Bush's Third Crusade Against the Muslims," 20 April 2002, http://www.mindspring .eu.com/thirdcrusade.htm; [Hizb ut-Tahrir], "America's Domination of the International Situation Is a Danger to the World and Only the Khilafah Can Save It," http://www.islamic-state.org/leaflets/ 030524_AmericasDominationOfWorldIsDanger.html.

57. Qur'an 9:123.

58. See, e.g., Waleed Gubara, "Speaking the Truth," *Khilafah Magazine* (May 2003): 26–28.

59. See "Bin Laadin Speaks on Hijrah; And The Islamic Emirate of Afghanistan."

60. I.e., Sahib, *Zaad e Mujahid*, 50–51; "Qiyam ul Lail: The Battle of Badr Compared to the Battle for Chechnya;" www.shu.ac.uk, "And Kill Them Wherever You Find Them, and Turn Them Out from Where They Have Turned You Out," 31 March 2002, http://www .islamic-state.org/leaflets/020331_AndKillThemWhereever YouFindThem.php.

61. The group that assassinated Sadat certainly felt this way. See, e.g., "Translation of Muhammad 'Abd al-Salam Faraj's Text Entitled 'Al-Faridah al-Gha'ibah,'" in Jansen, *The Neglected Duty*, 192–193.

62. Muhammad El-Halaby, "The Role of Sheikh-ul Islam Ibn Taymiyah in Jihad Against the Tatars," *Nida'ul Islam*, no. 17; see also "Ruling by Other Than What Allah Revealed; Tauheed Al-Hakkimyah," *Al-Jihaad*, No. 11, http://www.shareeah.com/Eng/aj/aj11.html; Shaykh Abu Muhammad al-Maqdisi, *This Is Our Aqidah!*, n.p., n.d., 28.

63. "Betrayed By Sheikh Uthaimin; Saudi Continue to Show Their Loyalty to Taghut," *Al-Jihaad*, no. 4.

64. Although there are several other groups that are equally vehement about killing the "false" Islamic rulers. See, i.e., "Ramadhan Message," *As-Sahwa*, November 2001, 3.

65. "The Despicable Submission of the Rulers Before the Open American Aggression," http://www.islamic-state.org/leaflets/030129_Despicable SubmissionOfRulersBeforeAmericanAggression.php; [Hizb ut-Tahrir], "Destroy the Fourth Crusader War," 20 March 2003; Haydar Ali Khan, "A Shift in Relations Between America & Saudi Arabia," *Khilafah Magazine* 15, no. 3 (March 2002): 11–12.

66. Ahmer Sajid, "The Treachery of the Rulers of Muslims in the 4th Crusade," *Khilafah Magazine* (April 2003): 12–13.

67. [Hizb ut-Tahrir], "And Kill Them Wherever You Find Them, and Turn Them Out from Where They Have Turned You Out."

68. Hizb-ut-Tahrir, *How the Khilafah Was Destroyed.*

69. Ibn Taimiyya, *Ibn Taimiyya on Public and Private Law in Islam: or Public Policy in Islamic Jurisprudence*, trans. Omar A. Farrukh (Beirut, Lebanon: Khayats, 1966), 142–148; see also such anti-Shi'a rhetoric as Khutbah of 9 June 2000, delivered at Finsbury Park Mosque by Sheikh Abu Hamza, "She Died a Mujaahida; Killing 27 Russian Soldiers," *Al-Jihaad*, no. 4; "Groups Of Shi'a; Are They Muslim?" *Al-Jihaad*, no. 4.

70. Ibn Taimiyya, *Ibn Taimiyya on Public and Private Law in Islam*, 142–148.

71. [Hizb ut-Tahrir], *How the Khilafah Was Destroyed.*

72. "Excerpts: 'Al-Qaeda' Tape Threatens Attacks," http://news.bbc.co.uk/ 2/hi/middle_east/3605593.stm.

73. http://www.iberiannotes.blogspot.com/2004_04_11_iberiannotes_ archive.html#108193744360327580.

74. Sahib, *Zaad e Mujahid*, 99–101.

75. Moulana Mohammed Masood Azhar, *The Virtues of Jihad* [Ahle Sunnah Wal Jama'at], n.p., n.d., 103ff.

76. "The Full Version of Osama bin Laden's Speech," *MEMRI Special Dispatch—Jihad and Terrorism Studies Project*, Middle East Media Research Institute, no. 811, 5 November 2004.

8. *Jihadist Ideology and the War on Terror*

1. For just some of the comparisons between this war and the Crusades, see Tayseer Allouni with Usamah bin Laden, "The Unreleased Interview, 21 October 2001," from Markaz Derasat (translated by Muawiya ibn Abi Sufyan), http://www.islamicawakening.com/index.htm? (http://www.as-sahwah.com); "Verdict Concerning the Disbelief of Those Who Assist United States Against the Muslims of Iraq," trans. Abu Qatada, http://www.gsmpro.com/article/articledt.asp?hArticleId= 991; Al-Sharq Al-Awsat, "Extracts from Al-Jihad Leader Al-Zawahiri's New Book 'Knights Under the Prophet's Banner,'" Foreign Broadcast Information Service (FBIS) translation, Document Number: FBIS-NES-2001-1202, 2 December 2001, parts 6 and 11; 'Usama bin Ladin, "On the Crusader War and the United Nations," 3 November 2002, http://www.jihadunspun.com/BinLadensNetwork/statements/ ootcwatun.cfm; 'Usama bin Ladin, "Discourse on Unity," March 2003, n.p.; 'Usama bin Ladin, "Audio Message," 11 February 2004, http://news.bbc.co.uk/2/hi/middle_east/2751019.stm; [Hizb al-Tahrir], "Destroy the Fourth Crusader War." See also David Zeidan, "The Islamic Fundamentalist Vision of Life as a Perennial Battle," *Middle East Review of International Affairs* 5, no. 4 (December 2001): 34–36.

2. Sayyid Qutb, *In the Shade of the Qur'an [Fi Zilal al-Qur'an]*, vol. 2 (Markfield, Leicester: The Islamic Foundation, 2000), 159.

3. Sayyid Qutb, *In the Shade of the Qur'an [Fi Zilal al-Qur'an]*, vol. 4 (Markfield, Leicester: The Islamic Foundation, 2001), 81–82, 88.

4. For a good discussion of the genesis of the takfiri movement, see Gilles Kepel, *Muslim Extremism in Egypt. The Prophet and Pharaoh* (Berkeley: University of California Press, [1984] 2003).

5. One of the most striking examples of this takfiri attitude can be found in Center for Islamic Studies and Research, "The Operation of 11 Rabi al-Awwal: The East Riyadh Operation and Our War with the United States and Its Agents," FBIS translation, n.p., n.d. See also "Verdict Concerning the Disbelief of Those Who Assist the United States Against the Muslims of Iraq"; Omar Bakri Muhammad, "Fatwa Against Those Who Ally with the Disbelievers Against Muslims," 11 September 2003, http://www.vcsun.org/~battias/911/20031000/20030911 .fatwa.txt; Abu 'Abd Al-Rahman Al-Athari Sultan Ibn Bijad, "An Open Letter from a Saudi Islamist to Those Who Shirk Jihad," Middle East Media Research Institute (hereafter MEMRI), *MEMRI Special Dispatch—Saudi Arabia/Jihad and Terrorism Studies Project*, no. 820, 30 November 2003.

6. The name of the al-Qaida linked Algerian group, Jama'a al-Salafiyya li'l-Dawa wa'l Jihad is but one expression of this belief.

7. See 'Usama Bin Muhammad Bin Ladin, "Declaration of War Against the Americans Occupying the Land of the Two Holy Places (Expel the Infidels from the Arab Peninsula)," *The Idler* 3, no. 165 (13 September 2001); 'Usama bin Ladin, "Text of Osama Bin Laden's Audio Message," 11 February 2003, www.homelandsecurity.com/obltext.asp.

8. John Miller, "To Terror's Source: John Miller's 1998 Interview with Osama Bin Laden," http://abcnews.go.com/sections/world/ DailyNews/miller_binladen_980609.html.

9. 'Usama bin Ladin, "A New Bin Laden Speech," July 18, 2003, Middle East Media Research Institute (hereafter MEMRI); 'Usama bin Ladin,

"Bin Laden's Sermon for the Feast of the Sacrifice," MEMRI, Special Dispatch Series, no. 476, March 2003.

10. 'Usama bin Ladin, "Bin Laden's Sermon for the Feast of the Sacrifice," MEMRI, Special Dispatch Series, no. 476, March 2003.

11. Tayseer Allouni with Usamah bin Laden, "The Unreleased Interview, 21 October 2001"; 'Usama bin Ladin, "Text of Osama Bin Laden's Audio Message"; John Miller, "To Terror's Source: John Miller's 1998 Interview With Osama Bin Laden"; al-Jazeera, "Full Text of bin Ladin Speech," 1 November 2004, http://english.aljazeera.net/NR/exeres/79C6AF22-98FB-4A1C-B21F-2BC36E87F61F.htm; Jamal Isma'il, "Transcript of Usamah bin Ladin, 'The Destruction of the Base,'" 10 June 1999, http://www.terrorism.com/modules.php?op=modload&name=News&file=article&sid=12&mode=thread&order=0&thold=0; see also Al-Sharq Al-Awsat, "Extracts from Al-Jihad Leader al-Zawahiri's New Book 'Knights Under the Prophet's Banner,'" FBIS translation, 2 December 2001, part 2.

12. That this was the explicit policy of the United States can be seen in George W. Bush, "Speech at National Defense University, 8 March 2005."

13. The war on the financial support for jihadis is covered by Matthew Levitt, "Combating Terrorist Financing: Where the War on Terror Intersects the 'Roadmap,'" *Jerusalem Issue Brief* 3, no. 4 (Jerusalem: Jerusalem Center for Public Affairs, 14 August 2003). For the actions taken by the United States since 9/11, see Michael G. Oxley, ed., *Dismantling the Financial Infrastructure of Global Terrorism: Hearing Before the Committee on Financial Services, U.S. House of Representatives* (Diane Publishing, 2003).

14. One of the most assiduous practitioners of this sort of da'wa is Hizb al-Tahrir.

15. Freedom House, *Saudi Publications on Hate Ideology Fill American Mosques* (Washington, DC: Center For Religious Freedom, 2005), 57ff.

16. The recent struggle between moderate and extremist Muslims over a mosque in Tennessee is but one example of the underlying conflict occurring not just in the United States but around the world over who will define Islam.

17. See the name that they chose for their organization: The World Islamic Front for Jihad Against the Jews and the Crusaders.

18. See, e.g., "The Religious Roots of the Upcoming US War," *As-Sahwa* 10, no. 1 (January/March 2003); 'Usama bin Ladin, "Bin Laden's Sermon for the Feast of the Sacrifice"; 'Usama bin Ladin, "Audio Message."

19. Ghaida Ghantous, "Zawahri Urges Muslims to Hit U.S. Allies' Interests," 1 October 2004, http://story.news.yahoo.com/news?tmpl=story2&u=/nm/20041001/wl_nm/security_qaeda_zawahri_dc.

20. See Ayman al-Zawahri's acknowledgment of this in Al-Sharq Al-Awsat, "Extracts from Al-Jihad Leader al-Zawahiri's New Book 'Knights Under the Prophet's Banner,'" part 11.

21. See, e.g., J. Kahn and T. Weiner, "World Leaders Rethinking Strategy on Aid to Poor," *New York Times*, 18 March 2002, sec. A(1), 3.

22. Alberto Abardie, "Poverty, Political Freedom and the Roots of Terrorism," in *Faculty Research Working Papers, October 2004* (Cambridge, MA: John F. Kennedy School of Government, 2004).

Glossary

Italicized words appearing in definitions are themselves defined in the glossary.

'aqida	doctrine
asbab al-nuzul	the "occasions of revelation," which provide the context that helps Islamic scholars to understand how to interpret the Qur'an
batil	literally "falsehood": the falsehood that opposes Islam
dar al-harb	the "house of war" that constitutes all territory not part of the *dar al-Islam*
dar al-Islam	the "house of Islam" that constitutes the entire Islamic community

da'wa	literally "call": the call to Islam and thus, more broadly, missionary work
din	religion
fard 'ayn	in Islamic law, a duty that is incumbent upon every Muslim
fard kifayya	in Islamic law, a duty that is considered fulfilled if some Muslims are carrying it out
fiqh	Islamic jurisprudence
hadith (pl. ahadith)	the traditions about the life of Muhammad which, together with the Qur'an and *sira*, constitute the source for the *sunna*
hakimiyyat Allah	the sovereignty of God
haqq	literally "truth": another term for Islam
haram	forbidden by Islamic law
harb	war
hijra	the Hegira or migration by Muhammad from Mecca to Medina, which constitutes the founding moment of Islam
hizb	a party
'ibada	worship
ijtihad	judicial reasoning
jahiliyya	literally "ignorance": the lack of knowledge about the true religion that dominated the world before Muhammad began his mission
jama'a	a group; also, the group prayer held on Fridays that is obligatory for all Muslims

jihad	(sacralized) struggle
jizya	the poll tax or tribute which, according to traditional views of shari'a, nonbelievers must pay in an Islamic state
kafir (pl. kuffar)	unbeliever
Khalifa	Caliph
khawarij	early heterodox Muslims who practiced takfir
Khilafa	the Islamic Caliphate
kufr	unbelief
mujahid (pl. mujahidun)	someone who participates in jihad
mulukiyya	monarchy
naskh	abrogation (of religious texts)
nizam	system
nusra	backing or protection
qital	fighting
al-Rashidun	literally "the Righteous Ones:" the first four Caliphs in Islamic history, viewed as especially pious
Salaf	the pious "predecessors," including the Companions of Muhammad (the Sahaba), the early Muslims who followed them, and the scholars of the first three generations of Muslims
salafi	in general any orthodox Muslim, but used

	currently to refer to the Wahhabis and related Islamists
shahada	the statement of faith ("There is no God but God and Muhammad is His Prophet") that all Muslims affirm
shari'a	Islamic law
shirk	polytheism; to declare that God has partners
sira	sacralized biographies of the life of Muhammad
sunna	"way" or "custom" of Muhammad; the sunna defines the proper manner that other Muslims should live their lives. Because so much of the information about Muhammad's life come from the hadith, the two terms are sometimes used interchangeably.
tafsir	commentary on the Qur'an or hadith
taghut	tyranny, oppression, or idolatry
takfir	to declare someone an apostate or unbeliever
tawhid	the central Islamic belief, as stated in the sha-hada, that there is only one God and He has no partners
tawhid al-rububiyya	the Lordship of God
umma	the Islamic community
usul al-fiqh	the four sources of Islamic law: the Qur'an, hadith, analogy, and consensus (of the ulama)
yasa	Mongol law

Index

Abbasids, 9, 10
Abduh, Muhammad, 28
Abou El Fadl, Khaled, 46, 47
abrogation (naskh), 44, 46, 54
Afghani, Sayyid Jamal al-Din al-, 28
Afghanistan, 3, 38, 39, 49, 114, 115,
    131, 148, 149, 153, 164, 165, 168,
    169, 171
Africa, 3, 6, 113
Ahmadis, 38, 157
Algeria, 96, 155
Ali, 24
Ali, Tariq, 5
al-Qaida, 2–4, 14, 50, 68, 72, 76, 77,
    96, 103, 115, 123, 128, 129, 133,
    152, 154, 160, 163, 164, 167, 168,
    173, 174
Americans, 1–3, 6, 7, 14, 35, 77, 91,
    96, 97, 100, 103, 104, 113, 123–25,
    128, 131, 147, 158, 167, 173

aqida (creed), 57, 58, 138
Arabian peninsula, 23, 25, 70, 104,
    168
Arabs, 2, 5, 36, 62, 99, 140
asbab al-nuzul (occasions of revela-
    tion), 53, 54
Assad, Bashar al-, 9, 34
Atatürk, Mustafa Kemal, 11, 28, 94,
    95
Atta, Muhammad, 6
Austria, 115
Awaji, Muhsin al-, 133
Azhar, Masood, 129, 131, 159
'Azzam, 'Abdullah, 114–16, 131,
    152

Badr, Battle of, 50, 141
Bali, 128
Balkans, 115
Bamyan Buddhas, 24

Banna, Hasan al-, 18, 27, 33–35,
   36–42, 52, 57, 93, 114, 120, 136,
   137, 139
batil. See falsehood
Beirut, 14, 103, 168
Berg, Nicholas, 129
Berlusconi, Silvio, 87
Bin Baz, 'Abd al-'Aziz, 103
bin Ladin, 'Usama, 46, 50, 67, 70, 71,
   74, 76, 86, 91, 96, 98, 100, 102,
   104, 112, 113, 119, 123, 128, 131,
   132, 143, 149, 152, 154–56, 158,
   159, 162, 165, 168, 169, 173
Blair, Tony, 87
booty, 126, 131, 133
Bosnia, 104
British, 26, 29, 33, 37, 69, 88, 94, 96,
   137
Bulgaria, 115
Bush, George W., 1, 87, 115
Byzantine Empire, 86, 88

Caliph, 9–11, 108, 129, 149, 151,
   152, 155
Caliphate (Islamic state), 4, 8, 11, 13,
   28, 31, 38, 39, 52, 64, 67, 77, 86,
   90, 94, 95, 113, 114, 121, 130, 131,
   138, 141, 142, 144, 145, 147–53,
   164, 168
capitalism, 12, 18, 30, 54, 65, 69, 75,
   76, 79
Chechnya, 104, 153, 155
Christian, 9, 12, 74, 92, 94
Christianity, 71, 79, 93
Christians, 8, 12, 21, 36, 43, 44, 47,
   67, 72, 80, 81, 86–91, 93, 103, 108,
   115, 119, 135, 155, 160
colonization, 5, 6, 18, 29, 30, 88, 95

communism, 32, 39, 60, 65, 69, 95
Conservative party, 73
conspiracy theories, 36, 54, 89, 95, 117
Copts, 155
Crimea, 115
Crusades, 88–92, 97
crusaders, 12, 26, 91, 112, 137, 145,
   165, 167, 169, 173

dar al-harb (House of War), 83, 166
dar al-Islam (House of Islam), 83
da'wa (the call to Islam), 30, 31, 33,
   139, 142, 143, 150, 167, 172, 173
decolonization, 18
democracy, 1, 36, 52, 54, 61, 67,
   72–74, 79, 92, 93, 96, 135, 162,
   177
Democratic party, 73
democratization, 177
din (religion), 68, 147
disbelief, 71

Egypt, 3, 26, 31, 33–35, 88, 114, 120,
   148, 155
Egyptian, 29, 33, 35, 37, 50, 67–69,
   128, 131, 148, 152
Europe, 9, 10, 12, 13, 18, 26, 30, 74,
   86, 92, 172
Europeans, 6, 9, 26, 29, 91, 92, 94,
   97, 169

Fahd ibn 'Abd al-'Aziz al-Sa'ud, 70
falsehood, 11, 13, 14, 21, 66, 80,
   84–86, 89, 121, 141, 162, 173
Faraj, Abdel Salam al-, 131
fascism, 32, 39
fatwa, 74
fiqh. See Islamic jurisprudence

First World War, 26
Fodio, Usman dan, 6
France, 26, 97, 173
freedom, 61, 62, 77–79, 92, 111, 129,
    162, 176, 177
French, 26, 88, 94, 103
French Revolution, 72
fundamentalism, 4, 101, 181, 183,
    184, 185, 186, 189, 190, 205

Geneva Convention, 129
Germans, 177
Germany, 26
Ghazzali, Abu Hamid Muhammad al-,
    54
GIA (Armed Islamic Group), 156
globalization, 1
Great Britain, 26, 73, 97, 148, 173
Greek thought, 10
GSPC (Salafist Group for Da'wa and
    Fighting), 156

hadith, 3, 10, 17–20, 23, 28, 29,
    41–48, 50–57, 67, 75, 81, 84–87,
    90, 93, 99, 101, 107–10, 116, 122,
    124, 125, 129, 131, 132, 136–38,
    143, 144, 151, 156, 159, 161
Hague Convention, 129
Hajj, 45
hakimiyyat Allah, 38, 61, 70
Hamas, 34, 37, 52, 72, 90, 93, 130,
    174
Hanbali, 19, 22, 24, 26, 107
Hanifi, 107, 130
Hawali, Shaikh Safar al-, 115
hijackers, 2, 3, 5, 124
hijra (migration), 44, 140, 142,
    144–49, 152, 153, 168

Hinduism, 79
Hindus, 7, 37, 44, 67, 135, 159, 160
Hizb al-Tahrir, 13, 57, 68, 71–73, 75,
    77, 78, 90, 92, 96, 112, 113, 115,
    125, 131, 143, 144, 146, 147, 150,
    152, 153, 156, 157
Hizbu'llah, 33
Hizbul-Mujahideen, 37
Hudaybiyya, Treaty of, 130
human rights, 18, 78, 126, 162
Hungary, 115
Huntington, Samuel, 83
Hussain, Saddam, 104

Ibn Khaldun, 'Abd al-Rahman, 54
Ibn Taymiyya, Ahmad ibn 'Abd
    al-Halim, 17, 19–24, 26, 28, 54,
    60, 67, 89, 136, 154, 156, 157
ijtihad, 10, 12
imperialism, 1, 5, 12, 18, 26, 88,
    91–93, 96, 97
India, 37, 100, 114–17, 141, 155, 160
Indians, 128, 129, 177
Indonesia, 3, 39, 104, 113
interfaith dialogue, 79, 101
International Monetary Fund (IMF),
    68
Intifada, 34
Iran, 3, 39, 50
Iraq, 3, 67, 99, 102, 113, 153, 155,
    156, 158, 167, 169
Islam, 2–17, 11, 19, 20, 23–25,
    27–33, 35–38, 41, 42, 44, 47, 48,
    51, 54–62, 64–66, 68, 69, 72–74,
    76, 78–95, 97, 99–101, 103–5,
    108, 110–13, 116–22, 124, 129,
    130, 132–43, 148–51, 154, 156,
    157, 162–67, 173, 177

Islamic community, 9–12, 18, 21, 26, 27, 30, 33, 42, 49, 50, 52, 67, 79, 85, 88, 90, 91, 94, 96–98, 100–102, 109, 110, 114, 122, 123, 132, 133, 141, 147, 151, 158, 160, 165, 169

Islamic Jihad (Egyptian), 152

Islamic jurisprudence, 19, 43, 67, 107, 112, 116, 122, 127, 131, 138

Islamic law, 9, 11, 13, 17, 19–23, 36, 38, 43, 47, 59, 63–65, 67–70, 73, 74, 95, 96, 104, 108, 111, 116, 122, 124–26, 133, 136, 138, 144, 146, 147, 149, 150, 152, 162, 163, 170, 171

Islamic scholars. See ulama

Islamic state. See Caliphate (Islamic state)

Islamism, 4, 29, 30, 34

Islamists, 4, 19, 38, 39, 52, 53, 72, 86, 102, 110, 112

Israel, 1, 6, 9, 34, 77, 91, 97, 98, 99, 102, 130, 155–57, 160, 173, 174

Israelis, 103, 124, 125, 128

Italy, 26

jahiliyya, 35, 38, 39, 65, 66, 69, 71, 141, 142, 145, 148

Jama'at ud-Dawa, 115

Jama'at-i-Islami, 37–39

Japan, 9

Jaylani, Muhammad al-, 6

Jewish, 51, 86, 92, 95, 98, 99, 137, 157

Jews, 8, 12, 13, 21, 36, 43, 44, 47, 50, 51, 67, 72, 76, 77, 80, 81, 85–89, 93, 94, 96, 98, 103, 108, 119, 135, 159, 160, 167, 173

jihad, 5, 7, 8, 13, 20, 21, 24, 31, 33, 34, 36, 37, 39, 41, 45, 49, 52–54, 67, 77, 105–22, 126–28, 130–32, 135, 136, 139, 144, 147, 149, 150, 152, 153, 157, 166, 168, 174

jihadis, 4, 5, 7–19, 22, 24, 25, 29, 38–47, 49, 50, 52–54, 57–60, 63, 64, 66, 67, 71–104, 107–10, 112–27, 129–38, 143–50, 154–59, 161–65, 167–77

jihadism, 6, 35, 42, 79, 102, 142, 175

jihadist discourse, 37, 48, 120

jihadist groups, 11, 12, 13, 21, 25, 34, 50, 57, 65, 67, 68, 74, 75, 77, 85, 88, 89, 98, 110, 120, 125, 132, 136, 137, 142, 148, 150, 152, 153, 155, 160, 166, 167, 174

jihadist ideologues, 9, 11, 18, 22, 25, 28, 29, 38–42, 48, 57, 112, 119, 121, 136, 142, 143

jihadist ideology, 5, 18, 29, 36, 47, 57–81, 161, 173, 176, 177

jihadist thought, 38, 45, 54, 76, 142, 162

jizya. See tribute

Johnson, Paul, 129

Jordan, 34, 96, 155

Judaism, 79

Jund al-Islam, 67

Justice and Development Party, 4

Kashmir, 37, 104, 114, 115, 153, 155

khawarij, 175

Khilafa. See Caliphate (Islamic state)

Khobar, 168

Khomeini, Ayatollah Ruhollah, 50, 52, 98

kufr. See unbelief

Labour party, 73
Lebanese, 103
Lebanon, 115, 155, 159
Leninism, 39
Levant, the, 26, 169
liberalism, 27, 36, 38, 42, 54, 71, 72, 75–77, 79, 80, 83–86, 89, 92, 93, 105, 135, 158, 162
liberty, 78, 79
Lobbo, Shehu Ahmadu, 6

Madrid, 115, 128, 158
Maliki, 107, 130
Maronites, 103
Marx, Karl, 60
Masri, Abu Hamza al-, 43, 69, 125, 132, 143, 145, 148, 156
Mawdudi, Sayyid Abul A'la, 18, 27, 29, 36–42, 37, 57, 59–62, 64, 67, 68, 73, 78, 110, 111, 119, 120, 136, 137, 143
Mecca, 44, 79, 140–42, 144
Medina, 140, 141, 144, 147, 149
Middle East, 1, 6, 34, 91, 97, 99, 113, 155, 177
modernism, 31, 69
modernization, 5, 18, 27
Mogadishu, 168
Mohammad, 'Umar Bakri, 73, 79, 84, 113, 130, 144, 148, 152
Mongols, 19, 22, 28, 136, 154, 165
Mubarak, Husni, 9, 96
Muhajiroun, al-, 43, 74, 78, 92, 113, 143, 148
Muhammad, 8, 11, 17–19, 21, 23, 24, 30–32, 36, 44, 45, 48, 50, 51, 53, 58, 62, 64, 65, 67, 75, 76, 79, 80, 84–89, 99, 101, 108, 109, 120, 124,

125, 130, 136–47, 149, 151, 153, 158, 166, 175
mujahidun, 109, 117, 125, 131, 159, 163, 165, 169
Mullah Omar, 149
Musharraf, Pervez, 9, 96
Muslim Brotherhood, 33–35, 37, 38, 68, 74
Muslim League, 73
Muslims, 2–5, 7–14, 17–26, 28, 30–34, 36–48, 50–54, 60, 63, 64, 66, 68–71, 74, 80, 83–96, 98–104, 109–18, 120–31, 135–42, 144–49, 151–54, 156–58, 160, 162–67, 172–77; apostate, 7, 21, 22, 37, 76, 108, 110, 118, 135, 137, 153, 154, 156, 157, 158, 175; fundamentalist, 101; heretical, 11, 21, 22, 24, 28, 31, 47, 54, 135, 136, 155, 157, 158, 175; liberal, 27, 42, 45, 47, 54, 110, 164, 173; moderate, 42, 45, 47, 54, 55, 101, 118, 164, 173; traditional, 164
Mustafa, Shukri Ahmad, 148
Muttahida Majlis-i-Amal (MMA), 38

Napoleon, 26
naskh. See abrogation
Nasser, Gamal Abdel, 35
nationalism, 18, 27, 29, 42, 73, 101, 135, 150
New York, 103, 158

orientalism, 99
orientalists, 93, 94
Ottoman Caliphate, 11, 149
Ottoman Empire, 10, 22, 26, 96
Ottomans, 22, 23

Pakistan, 73, 96, 114, 115, 155, 158
Pakistanis, 131
Palestine, 34, 98, 102, 114, 115, 155, 174
Palestinian Authority, 102
Palestinian-Israeli conflict, 173, 174
Palestinians, 103, 124
Pearl, Daniel, 129
Pharaoh, 50, 87, 165
Poland, 115
polygamy, 27
polytheism, 68, 69
polytheists, 44, 67, 108, 145, 159
poverty, 1, 5, 13
prisoners of war, 45, 123, 125, 126, 128, 129, 133

Qaradhawi, Yusuf al-, 103, 128
Qur'an, 3, 8, 10, 17–21, 23, 28–33, 35, 41–57, 59, 67, 69, 75, 76, 79, 80, 84–87, 90, 93, 99, 101, 107, 109, 112, 116, 118, 122, 123, 125, 131, 132, 136–38, 141, 143, 144, 155, 161, 166
Quraysh, 141
Qutb, Sayyid, 6, 11, 18, 25, 29, 35, 36, 37, 38, 39, 41, 42, 51, 57–69, 71–73, 75, 77–79, 85, 86, 88, 91–94, 104, 110, 111, 117, 119, 121, 130, 132, 136, 137, 139–44, 165, 166

Ramadan, Tariq, 5
reconquista, 115
Republican party, 73
Rida, Muhammad Rashid, 18, 27–29, 42

Riyadh, 168
Romania, 115
Russia, 97, 116, 155
Russians, 125

Sadat, Anwar, 50, 128
Sahib, Mufti Khubiab, 159
Said, Edward, 5
Salaf, 27, 28, 43, 45
salafism, 25, 27
Salah al-Din, 90, 91, 165
Saudi Arabia, 5, 14, 24, 25, 49, 70, 102, 113, 115, 131, 148, 155, 158, 167
Saudis, 9, 14, 24, 76, 77
secularism, 7, 27, 28, 31, 33, 71–73, 75, 79, 92, 95, 120
September 11, 1–4, 6, 14, 49, 76, 98, 124, 128, 133, 161, 163–65, 168, 171, 173, 175
Shafi'i, 107, 108
Shah of Iran, 6, 50
Shah Wali Allah, 6
shahada, 58, 68
shari'a. See Islamic law
Shi'a, 24, 45, 157, 158
Shi'ism, 25
shirk. See polytheism
Siddiqi, Shamim, 145, 147, 148
Siddiqui, Kalim, 150
sira (sacralized biographies of Muhammad), 137–39, 143, 151, 158
slavery, 27
socialism, 18, 29, 30, 42, 60, 69, 73, 120
Somalia, 14, 104, 112, 155, 159, 168

Spain, 113, 115, 141, 173
Sudan, 39, 104, 114
Sufism, 3, 24, 25, 136
suicide bombers, 124, 125
sunna. See hadith
Sunnis, 19, 45, 116
Supporters of Shari'ah, 92, 148
Syria, 3, 34, 73

taghut (tyranny), 85, 87
takfir, 64, 70, 166, 167, 175
Taliban, 24, 25, 38, 39, 148, 149
Tatars, 116
tawhid, 23–25, 38, 39, 58–64,
    66–70, 78, 79, 119, 161, 162, 173
terrorism, 69, 101, 102, 126, 132, 133
terrorists, 4, 101, 168
tribute (jizya), 43, 108, 116, 130
Tunisia, 3
Turkey, 3, 4, 26
Turks, 28

ulama, 8, 10, 12, 17, 24, 26, 27, 39,
    42, 43, 46, 71, 72, 103, 109, 111,
    116, 128, 140, 145, 166
umma. See Islamic community
unbelief (kufr), 11–14, 68, 73,
    84–86, 88, 89, 95, 99, 104, 105,
    137, 146, 154, 155
unbelievers, 9, 11, 13–17, 19–22, 24,
    31, 32, 36, 37, 42, 43, 48, 50, 51,
    53, 64, 66, 67, 70, 77, 79, 81,
    84–88, 90, 91, 94–96, 99, 102,
    104, 107, 109, 112–19, 112, 114,
    118, 121, 124, 125, 127, 128,
    130–33, 135, 136, 137, 141, 142,

145–47, 149, 151, 152, 154, 155,
    158, 159, 166, 172, 173
United Nations, 54, 67, 68, 74, 78,
    104
United States, 1–7, 9, 10, 12–15, 18,
    35, 38, 39, 49, 50, 69, 70, 72–74,
    76, 77, 86, 89, 96–100, 102–4,
    112, 113, 119, 123, 147, 149,
    153–57, 159, 161, 162, 164,
    168–73, 175
usury, 75, 76, 145

Wahhab, Muhammad ibn 'Abd al-, 6,
    7, 18, 22–26, 28, 31, 36, 42, 67, 96,
    136, 157, 167
Wahhabis, 24, 102, 144, 173
Wahhabism, 25, 28
Washington, D.C., 2, 103, 159
West, the, 6, 7, 13, 15, 29, 30, 32, 35,
    36, 38, 39, 60, 69–72, 74, 75, 77,
    80, 81, 87, 88, 95, 97, 100–103,
    110, 112, 117, 123, 131, 135, 156,
    162, 166, 177
Westernization, 5, 30
Westphalia, Treaty of, 74
World Bank, 68

Yakan, Fathi, 68, 112

Zarqawi, Abu Musab al- (Ahmad
    Fadil al-Nazal al-Khalaylah), 25,
    158, 162, 167
Zawahri, Ayman al-, 46, 98, 123–25,
    152, 173
Zionism, 91
Zoroastrians, 108

Portland Community College